HELPING
YOUR
AGING PARENT

A Step-By-Step Guide

by

William J. Grote

Boomer Books
P.O. Box 2899, Vista, CA 92083

You Do Something Good When You Buy This Book!

A portion of your purchase will be donated to the National Council on the Aging.
The NCOA works with hundreds of community organizations to assist older people. It prepares them to find jobs, disseminates health information, and pushes federal legislation such as the Older Americans Act.

Special thanks to the people who made this book possible:

Bessie Grote, mom, who gave me the dream and believed that I could do anything if I tried hard enough (except fix my own car).

Elaine Grote-Mancarti, sister, who encouraged and tried to help put this together when no one could stand it.

Carole Grote-Breyer, stepmom, who tried to help me write, and probably figured I was hopeless.

Gary Moselle, book publisher, who showed me everything I know about publishing.

Genie Runyon, the editor who gave me encouragement in the beginning and showed me how to write.

Jennifer Filo, social worker of Elizabeth Hospice in Escondido, CA, who educated me on hospice.

Laurence Jacobs, the editor and friend who found the mistakes everyone else missed.

Lilly Hazelton, a financial consultant, who explained financial advice that was over my head.

Merritt Voigtlander, the art director who taught me style, and sent in clouds for the cover.

Mike Conlen, welder-man artist who can design a mean logo.

Paul Smith, of Scheafer & Smith, in Vista, CA – a lawyer who acts like a real person.

Ray and Toni Klapka, care managers, who taught me all about residential care facilities.

Rozanne Bryson, editor, who put up with the writing, pretended it had potential, and made it readable.

Tom Matteson, of Press Time printing, who has a heart as big as a web press.

Looking for other books like this?

Look in the order form in the back of this book for other books that will help you in your journey in taking care of your parent.

Illustrations by Matt Kim

Cover photo by Ed Kessler Photography

ISBN 0-9717373-0-4

Library of Congress Control Number 2002108733

© Copyright 2002 by Boomer Books

Contents

CHAPTER I

How Do You Know When Your Parent Needs Help?

Sooner or later most of us will have to step in and help our parents. Often, if you live near your parents and have a close relationship with them, you may just gradually fall into a pattern where you begin to take a larger and more active role in your parents' day-to-day life. But that's generally not the case. Most of us live busy, active lives, and our parents do too. Or so we may think – especially if our parents are still married or have remarried. We talk on the phone and visit as often as we can, but our lives are going in very different directions from our parents'. While we're speeding into middle age trying to make our mark on the world, raising our children and being productive adults with expanding horizons, our parents are slowing down. And too often, we don't even notice it until something happens and suddenly, one or both of our parents need our help.

When that occurs, many of us don't know where or how to begin. And in truth, we may not *want* to begin. After all, to take on the responsibility of caretaker to a parent is a difficult adjustment. This is the person who took care of you, the person you always depended on, the one you turned to when you needed help or advice or encouragement. Reversing that role isn't always easy – for either of you. You may both resist, or even deny, the need for as long as possible. I know from experience, because that's how it was with my mother and me. It takes time to get comfortable with the idea. Unfortunately, time may not be what you have.

My object in writing this book is to help you and your parents deal with this adjustment. My parents passed away within a few years of each other. My father died suddenly in a car accident, and my mother died slowly over the course of a year, and needed a great deal of care and assistance. You might think my father's

> "While we're speeding into middle age trying to make our mark on the world, raising our children and being productive adults with expanding horizons, our parents are slowing down. And too often, we don't even notice it until something happens and suddenly, one or both of our parents need our help."

death was easier to handle, but that's not the case at all. It was actually much more difficult because of its suddenness. There was no time for goodbyes. He was just gone. It made me aware that I needed to spend more time with my mother. And that was fortunate, because within a few years her health began to decline.

Being able to step in and help your parents when they're truly in need is one of the most important opportunities you'll have in your lifetime. It's far more important than a promotion at work, or any personal achievement you may seek for yourself. It's a chance to get in touch with the meaning of why you're here, to become aware of the greater sense of your humanity, or even allowing you insight into your role as a spiritual being. If you're faced with this situation, I urge you not to turn the opportunity away. In spite of the difficulties, you'll find rewards that will change the way you view life forever.

But first you have to convince yourself and your parents that there is a problem that needs your help.

Awakening to the Problem

My sister and I were used to a very independent mother. My parents were divorced for over 20 years, and my mother never remarried. She had a career, retired, did volunteer work, kept busy with friends and family, and seemed content to live alone. She was part of our lives, but had her own life. She was intelligent, capable, and self-reliant. We never thought it would ever be any different. I'm sure she felt that way as well. But over time she suffered several small strokes that damaged her memory and her reasoning. My sister and I were totally unaware that anything had happened to our mother. She just began to change. She seemed forgetful, a little confused, and showed some signs of paranoia. We thought it was part of getting older and denied to ourselves that there was anything really wrong. She didn't ask for help or tell us she was concerned that something was happening to her. She did, however, decide to move out of her home and into a senior retirement home.

> "My sister and I were totally unaware that anything had happened to our mother. She just began to change."

Then one day she fell and she didn't know what had happened to her. My sister took her to the doctor, who ran some tests, but the tests didn't show anything significant. We let things go for a while, but gradually my sister and I realized that our mother's mental abilities were deteriorating. She was more and more forgetful. We thought she wasn't taking her blood pressure medication, so we paid to have the nurse at the retirement home administer her pills daily. But that didn't seem to make a difference. Our mother needed help. We didn't know what to do or where to go – and we weren't getting any straight answers from her doctor. What we did know was that she was getting worse, not better. Finally, we were advised that through Medicare, our mother was eligible to have a geriatric screening at a local medical center. The examination was very thorough. She was diagnosed with dementia, a deterioration of the mental pathways caused by the strokes. She could no longer live alone.

There are some major barriers you may have to get past before you can provide a parent with the help he or she needs. First, both you and your parent have to admit there's a problem. Second, you have to overcome the invisible shield of authority that exists between parent and child. And last – and this may be really difficult for some – you have to be able to communicate openly with each other, and that may require some forgiveness on both sides.

Admitting the Need

Most of us tend to ignore the early signs of our parents' decline. Maybe we don't consciously ignore the signs, but rather just overlook them or convince ourselves they aren't there. We may not want to acknowledge the idea that our parents are declining, so we don't act until we are forced to. The reality may be brought to our attention by one of our parents' neighbors or friends when their concern prompts them to call and tell us our parent is behaving differently. Or maybe we aren't forced to act until our parent is in the hospital, or even at death's door.

"The reality may be brought to our attention by one of our parent's neighbors or friends when their concern prompts them to call and tell us that our parent is behaving in a strange manner."

Many seniors fiercely defend their independence by trying to shield their weaknesses from others. They often become closed off, emotionally withdrawn, or angry when confronted about their physical or mental decline. Sound like any one you know? Because of this desire to remain independent, your parent may avoid asking for the necessary help until it's too late. They may have difficulty handling the idea of you taking care of them. Some older people, especially older men, can be so darn stubborn that they never ask for help! When you finally become aware of the problem, your job will most likely be more difficult because the problem will be more acute. Maybe their legs are swollen and turning blue due to water retention. Or perhaps they've become diabetic. Maybe they haven't called you because their eyesight is failing and they can't read the numbers on the telephone. Osteoporosis may take away their bone strength, so a small fall on a broken step will cause a fractured hip and a stay in the hospital. And tragically, dementia can sneak in and you won't realize your parents are living in a confused state until you actually see the mess with your own eyes. When you finally arrive on the scene, you'll have to take charge of a situation that grew into a monster like the 'Blob' because both you and your parent ignored it when it was a small problem. And that can be disastrous.

Overcoming the Invisible Shield of Authority

Whether you realize it or not, there is a force that keeps you from probing into your parents' private life. It's like an invisible shield around them protecting them from your doubts about their competence. They are, after all, your parents – and usually the most important adult role models you've had in your life. For the first 20 or so years, they were pretty much in charge. They taught you right from wrong, took care of you, and helped you make many of the decisions that shaped you as an adult. They'll always be your parents, and you'll always be their child. There'll never be a complete reversal of the parent role. It's just that now you need to help them with major life decisions. And you may have to struggle to get through the invisible shield of authority that surrounds your image of them. Don't be afraid to take that step, but do remember that you're dealing with your parents – and always show them the respect and dignity they deserve.

Forgiveness - the Beginning of Healing

> "Studies show that people who can forgive others are happier and emotionally better adjusted than those who can't forgive."

You need to try and resolve any old issues you've held onto – especially if they prevent you from communicating freely and really connecting with one another. Take the opportunity to discuss old wounds so you can heal them. This will be good for both of you. Forgive your parents' past wrongs and ask them to forgive you, too. No one's perfect. At this stage in your life you may be able to admit they were doing the best they could – even though you felt wronged or neglected or even abused. And now that you're a parent, if you are, you can see that children aren't always easy to deal with. That's a good place to start.

It's funny how we magnify our hurts. They often become a disproportionate part of our memories. Sometimes they can completely take over our lives. Did you know that forgiveness actually induces healing? Studies show that people who can forgive others are happier and emotionally better adjusted than those who can't. According to clinical studies, the art of forgiveness can bring about major psychological and physical changes in the person doing the forgiving. Forgive your parent today. It'll do you both a world of good.

"You may be starting down a long and difficult journey together and it's important to start off on the right path."

You may be starting down a long and difficult journey together and it's important to start off on the right path. By resolving old conflicts you can smooth the road ahead and fill in those emotional potholes. If it's a difficult thing for you to do, try to break down the barriers gradually. Each time you visit your parents in the early stages of your caretaking, ease into conversations about how things were when you were growing up. It makes great after dinner, or before bedtime, conversation. It's important for you to take this step. It sets the groundwork for the steps that follow. Get to know your parents as people rather than as parents. Drag out the photo album and ask what they were thinking or feeling during different times in their life. Use this time as an opportunity to find out what their hopes and ambitions were, what they started out to do with their life, and what or who encouraged them to do what they did. It may be they're different from what you thought they were. You may find out you have a lot in common. You might even start to appreciate the sacrifices they made in their life, or at the very least, come to an understanding of some of the difficulties they faced. Forgiveness begins with understanding.

If you never had a great relationship with your parents, don't hold onto any illusion that they're going to suddenly become the dream parent you always wanted. That probably won't happen. Just try to accept them and love them for who they are now. You can't change the past, and they're not going to change radically at this stage of life. But you can change your expectations. You may only have this last period of their life to really get to know them. Take advantage of it.

Hopefully, the information that follows will help you recognize impending problems so you can take action and save your parent unnecessary pain and you unnecessary hardship and worry.

How to Determine if There's Really a Problem

You probably wouldn't be reading this book unless you've already noticed a change in your parents' behavior. Or maybe someone else has mentioned that something isn't right. It may not be anything you can put your finger on –– you just know that something doesn't look good or sound right about one of your parents. Here are a few things you might look out for.

General changes in habits or behavior

The most important thing to watch for is a change in regular habits or attitudes, such as their behavior toward you or others, their mood, their memory, their thinking or problem-solving ability, their breathing, appetite or sleeping habits, and their ability to handle everyday life. The symptoms can be very subtle. Note any changes in their behavior each time you visit, and try to visit more often. You may pick up on something before your parent does.

Forgetfulness and confusion

An obsession with writing notes and sticking them everywhere can be a signal that your parent's memory is fading. They may be using notes to compensate for an inability to remember commonly-used phone numbers, events, or even names. A calendar with days crossed off and numerous reminders written in may be another

"If you never had a great relationship with your parent, don't hold onto any illusion that they're going to suddenly become the dream parent you always wanted. That probably won't happen. Just try to accept them and love them for who they are now. You can't change the past, and they're not going to change radically at this stage of life. But you can change your expectations. You may only have this last period of their life to really get to know them. Take advantage of it."

"A calendar with days crossed off and numerous reminders written in may be another sign."

sign. If this is something they've always done, then it isn't a change. What you're looking for are signs of changing behavior.

Does your parent know when they took their medication last? Can they tell you what they ate at their last meal – or even if they ate? Have they forgotten where they put various items, including money? Do they forget routine appointments or dates, such as a weekly bridge game or lunch date? Are they afraid to drive alone? Or, if they take a bus, have they forgotten which bus they routinely take, or became confused and got off at the wrong stop? Do they call you over and over and ask the same question – without seeming to know they've called before?

Overdue bills

Overdue bills can be another warning sign. On the surface everything may seem normal, but their mind may be so taxed with what are to them overwhelming problems that they can't organize what they need to do. They can't decide what bills need to be paid or if they've already paid them – or what to do about renewing services or paying taxes or keeping up their insurance. Your first clue may be when their cable service, or worse, you're notified that their electricity is about to be turned off, and they don't know why.

Unfamiliar bills

This may be where your parent is most vulnerable. If they're confused or lonely, they can be prey to all kinds of schemes. Older people, especially those living alone, seem to attract hordes of phone solicitors and door-to-door salesmen. Sometimes the older person just enjoys the opportunity to talk to someone - and the next thing they know, they've bought something they don't need or can't even use. By the time the item arrives or they get the bill, they don't remember when, why, or how they bought it.

The car

For many older people, their car is a symbol of their independence. For you, it can also be a good barometer of how things are going. Are they driving less and less? Is the car in good repair? Is it kept clean and washed? How are the tires? Are they in good shape or have they gone bald and your parent hasn't seemed to notice? Is the insurance up-to-date? Check the registration. I found my mother had let her registration lapse two years before she finally decided to quit driving. It never even occurred to me to check. You might discover your parent hasn't been driving for some time. Maybe they flunked their driver's exam and didn't want to tell you. Or maybe they never took, it fearing they wouldn't pass, and just let their license lapse. Maybe they've been driving without a license.

Changes in hobbies

Has your parent lost interest in hobbies or social activities that used to be important to them? That's a good indication something is amiss. If your parent enjoyed a hobby such as oil painting, stamp collecting, playing bridge, or singing with the church choir, and has suddenly stopped for no apparent reason, something is up. A change is taking place that may soon require your action. This change is only a symptom of a larger problem. Pay attention – it may be just the tip of the iceberg.

Warnings from neighbors

Be especially concerned if your parent shows inappropriate responses towards other people, such as extreme anger, anxiety, or paranoia. This could be directed at a total stranger, a neighbor, a friend or family member, or even you. If they appear serious about what you think is an imagined threat, don't just disregard it. They may act on it. Look into it. Listen to what they say, and listen to what others say. If a neighbor takes you aside and explains that your parent has been acting strangely, and then proceeds to tell you some shocking tale that you find hard to believe, look into it! Elderly neighbors tend to look out for each other, so there may be some truth in what you're hearing. Remember the old adage "Where there's smoke, there's fire."

Physical warnings

There are some outward signs you can easily spot that indicate a serious health problem is forthcoming. Watch for a sore or wound that doesn't seem to heal – it could be more serious than you think. Is this sore on their face or arms? It could be skin cancer. Does your parent have incontinence? Do they have problems urinating or eliminating? Urinary tract infections are quite common in older people. And any type of infection in an older person, even an infection in their teeth or gums, can put a strain on other body systems. Look at the color of their skin. Do they have a healthful blush to their cheeks or are they pale? Is there a yellow or orange tint to their skin that could indicate jaundice? Are their eyes clear and bright or are they dull? Do they complain about clouded vision? Does your parent breathe hard after a short walk or have any swelling in their legs or ankles? What about tremors of any kind? Do their hands shake?

"There are some outward signs you can easily spot that indicate a serious health problem is forthcoming"

The Evaluation Checklist shown in Figure 1-1 is designed to help you evaluate your parents' need for help. Next to the type of symptom is the maximum number of points to allocate for that problem. If your parents' symptoms total more than 100 points, you need to take immediate action. If you've noticed any of the symptoms I've discussed or ones appearing on the checklist, take your parent to a doctor soon for a complete physical exam.

This form included on the disk in the back of this book.

Parent Health Evaluation Checklist

Major Signs of Decline   20 points each

Your parent had a medical emergency.   ☐   _____

Someone alerted you to a problem.   ☐   _____

Mental Changes   10 points each

Is there a change of mood?   ☐   _____

Have they given up a hobby?   ☐   _____

Are they less social?   ☐   _____

Are there notes everywhere?   ☐   _____

Are there unopened bills, mail, or papers lying around?   ☐   _____

Is their house orderly?   ☐   _____

Is the car being driven?   ☐   _____

Is the car maintained in good condition?   ☐   _____

Is the car insurance and registration current?   ☐

Are they behaving strangely toward neighbors,

friends or family?   ☐   _____

Other _____   ☐   _____

Other _____   ☐   _____

Physical Signs   10 points each

Do you see any obvious signs of health decline?   ☐   _____

Are they short of breath?   ☐   _____

Is their skin a normal tone?   ☐   _____

Are their legs or ankles swollen?   ☐   _____

Do they complain of new aches or pains?   ☐   _____

Do they have a new cough?   ☐   _____

Do they complain of headaches?   ☐   _____

Have they lost their appetite?   ☐   _____

Do they seem lethargic or unusually inactive?   ☐   _____

Other _____   ☐   _____

Other _____   ☐   _____

Total _____

Figure 1-1 Parent Health Evaluation Checklist

Make Sure Your Parent Sees a Doctor

As your parent gets older there are hundreds of things that can go wrong with their health. Any of the symptoms I've listed should serve as a wake-up call that your help is needed. If a health problem goes untreated and your parent refuses to address it, you'll have to overcome that invisible shield of authority, and get them to a doctor. Here are just a few of the typical health problems that affect older people.

Skin Problems

You may occasionally notice a reddish-brown or purple area on your parent's forearm. It can look as if your parent has been knocked around by a mysterious assailant. These marks are probably just bleeding under the skin caused by a simple bruise. This is common in older people. Their skin is thinner and usually has less cushioning against impacts. Most of these spots eventually disappear. But if they don't go away in a reasonable time, have the doctor check it out.

As the body ages, skin may become dry and itchy. If your parent has a constant itch, and their eyes or skin look yellowish, have the doctor check it out. It could be jaundice, or it could indicate several other conditions. It's a good reason to make an appointment to see the doctor.

Face Pains

If your parent has shooting pains down one side of their face they may have a condition called trigeminal neuralgia. This nerve can go haywire in older people, causing pain and occasional facial twitching. If you notice this happening to your parent, tell the doctor. There's medication to control it.

Painful Joints

If your parent has stiff, painful, or swollen joints in the hips, knees, and spine, especially in the morning, they may have osteoarthritis. This is the most common of all joint disorders, and practically everyone gets it eventually in some form or other if they live long enough. Usually an X-ray can determine if osteoarthritis is the cause of joint pain or if it is rheumatoid arthritis – another disease of the joints that usually only appears after the age of 40. While there is no magic cure for osteoarthritis, losing weight

Watch Out for Scam Artists

Shortly before my mother sold her home and moved into a retirement home, she signed a contract for a home improvement project that seemed a little odd and extremely expensive to me. The contract was for earthquake reinforcing for the foundation of her mobile home. The cost of the reinforcing was several times more than her mobile home was worth. I was even more suspicious about this project when I learned that she got the idea from a door-to-door salesman. I asked her if she would mind if I went over the contract with her. After discussing it with me, she realized she'd been talked into something she didn't need, had never thought about before, and really didn't want to commit to. She was a little embarrassed about it, but there was no harm done. She could get out of the contract under the three-day cancellation clause. And she did.

It's a good idea to ask your parent if you can go over any contracts with them before they sign. Tell them you might be able to save them some money. If your parent is like my mother, they'll appreciate your thoughtfulness and not think you're trying to snoop. Most retirees live on a fixed income, and will generally like the idea of a better deal. Examine every contract very carefully. This is a big responsibility for you. Once you've engaged your parent's trust, you must live up to the office.

If you find they've just signed a big contract for something really wacky, don't get angry. You'll make them feel foolish and you could lose their trust. Make a giant mental note to yourself that you need to pay more attention to them. You can usually get them out of the contract, if you act in time (In most states there's a three-day clause that gives them time to back out.) But, if you overreact, you might not get the chance to rescue them next time.

and exercising – like walking daily, will help. There are several drugs and over-the-counter products that may offer some relief. Acupuncture may also provide some relief. These remedies are much cheaper and less complicated than hip replacement surgery. Talk to the doctor about alternative treatments before resorting to surgery. Older people heal very slowly and are prone to complications from any surgical procedure.

Osteoporosis

This sneaky disease is seldom discovered until after your parent suffers a fall or injury, and then you find that their bones are barely holding them together. Elderly women are most susceptible to osteoporosis and it may be a hereditary condition. If your parent develops a backache or sudden severe back pain, make sure they see a doctor. A fracture of the spine could result in paralysis. Doctors can do a bone density test or X-ray the spine to check for osteoporosis. There's no definite cure for osteoporosis. Taking daily calcium supplements, along with vitamin D to help the body absorb the calcium, can help your parent develop stronger bones even after age 70. Exercise also helps sustain bone mass, especially exercise such as walking, riding a stationary bike, or lifting weights. Your parent may take this advice more seriously if they hear it from a doctor rather than from you.

> "Exercise also helps sustain bone mass, especially exercise like walking, riding a stationary bike, and lifting weights. Your parent may take this advice more seriously if they hear it from a doctor rather than you."

Severe Headache, Numbness, Vision, and Speech Difficulties

Watch for signs of a stroke. A stroke occurs as a result of disturbed blood flow to the brain. We've probably all heard the phrase "hardening of the arteries." The arteries become lined with a build-up of plaque that hardens and constricts the blood flow. Little pieces of this plaque can break away from the artery wall, get carried into the smaller blood vessels of the brain, become lodged there, and cut off the blood flow to that area. There are different degrees of strokes. Some are mild and the effects aren't even noticeable right away. Others are stronger and result in temporary numbness, slurred speech, dizziness, or a headache. These are more easily recognized and treated. More severe strokes can lead to temporary or permanent paralysis.

Small strokes can cause vascular dementia, a common condition among the elderly. It may take several strokes before the signs begin to appear. Larger strokes may only affect a portion of the brain and disable certain parts or functions of the body. The victim may black out and wake up to find they're unable to speak or move part of their body. Major strokes can cause massive hemorrhaging, and immediate or eventual death. Strokes and coronary artery disease are the largest single cause of death in the U.S. Both conditions are caused by roughened artery walls or by plaque that builds up on artery walls over the years. If your family has a history of strokes, this information should be included in your parent's medical records and you should have their blood cholesterol level checked by a doctor. Have your cholesterol checked too!

Fainting Spells

Fainting can be caused by many things, some serious, and some not so serious. If fainting is the result of a spinning sensation accompanied by a weak feeling in the arms or legs, a tingling feeling, or blurred vision, it could be a stroke. Get your parent to the doctor right away. If dizziness occurs when they suddenly stand up from a sitting or lying position, it's usually caused by a temporary drop in blood pressure, and is normal. If your parent is taking medication for high blood pressure, they may need to have their medication adjusted. Fainting or dizzy spells are dangerous because they can result in falls, causing more serious injuries, such as broken bones, that require surgery or prolonged hospital stays.

Swollen Ankles

Swollen ankles can indicate water retention, early stages of kidney failure, or congestive heart failure. Even though it sounds ominous, congestive heart failure is not immediately life-threatening if treated. There are prescription drugs that lessen the symptoms. If your parent has swollen ankles, get them to a doctor as soon as possible, and make sure the doctor provides a remedy for the problem.

Urinary Problems

If your parent seems fatigued and complains of vague pain, check the toilet. Cloudy or smelly urine can indicate a urinary tract infection. Left untreated, a urinary tract infection can bring older people seemingly to the edge of existence. This type of infection is easy to cure with sulfa or antibiotics. Usually one doctor visit can do the trick. But don't let it go untreated!

If you notice the smell of urine when your parent is around, or you see a spot on their clothing that indicates they've had an accident, they may be suffering from incontinence. You need to have a private talk with them about their inability to control their bladder. As much as we dislike doing this, it's worse if you don't. They may not realize that anyone can tell, and it's much better if it comes from you than someone else! Tell them that it's a common problem. As a matter of fact, over 30 percent of people over the age of 60 have some degree of incontinence. Fortunately, it's not a life threatening condition, although it can lead to embarrassment, loss of dignity, and depression if not taken care of. Before you break out the adult diapers, however, ask your doctor to recommend a urologist who specializes in geriatric patients. Sometimes they can prescribe drugs and exercises to help an older patient regain control of their bladder. If you're not satisfied your parent is getting appropriate care, check into getting help at a geriatric care center. Some have special clinics designed to aid seniors with incontinence.

> "Fainting or dizzy spells are dangerous because they can result in falls, causing more serious injuries, such as broken bones, that require surgery or prolonged hospital stays."

When to Step In and Take Charge

Even though you see the signs of decline, sometimes it's difficult to insert your-self into your parent's life. You may think you don't have the right to step in and start making decisions for them. Here are a few suggestions.

Start Talking - the Sooner the Better

Talk with your parent. Both of you need to come to terms with the fact that they need your help, if not now, in the near future. Keep in mind that they may be reluctant to face their problems, especially straight on. You may have to ease into the discussion. If your attempt to bring the subject up is always headed off at the pass with "Let's talk about this later" or "Things aren't that bad," change your approach. Pretend you just read an interesting article in the newspaper or on the Internet or heard something on the radio that relates to what you want to discuss. Or pretend you're talking about a friend's parent. Then ask your parent their opinion about the story.

> "Be gentle but firm in your efforts to discuss these issues. Don't give up."

If this approach doesn't work, talk about your parent's parents. Do you remember what their relationship was like with your grandparents? Did they have to take care of their parents? What happened? Find out if they've given any thought to long-term health care. Get them thinking and talking about it. Get it out in the open, where you can discuss the future. Ask them if they've considered making out a will or a trust? Be gentle but firm in your efforts to discuss these issues. Don't give up. Tell them you want to take them to the doctor – just for a checkup. Tell them you love them, and you're there to help because you're concerned.

Enlisting Your Family Members' Help

Sometimes a parent is more likely to share certain thoughts or ideas with another family member than you. Don't feel bad about this. Feel great! The more ways you can enlist others to help, the less you'll have to do on your own. Better to share this burden with all your family members. Sometimes feelings of resentment at carrying the full responsibility of a parent's care can split a family apart. Try not to let that happen. It won't help your parent. They'll need everyone's help and sup-port. We're all endowed with a separate set of gifts. When it comes to helping a parent, everyone has something they can offer, and it may be completely different from what you can do. Utilize the whole arsenal by getting everyone involved. If your parent has assets, it's in everyone's best interest to protect those assets by work-ing together. If your parent doesn't have assets, it's in your parent's best interest for you all to work together to provide the best housing, health care, and attention that you can. After all, isn't that what they gave you?

Pull your family members together and establish a family committee to get everyone involved in making decisions regarding your parent's care. A majority vote should do. Don't let one family member try to dominate your decisions or pull you all into a stalemate. Figure 1-2 is a Family Enlistment Form. Have every family member agree to it, sign it, and return it to you. Then make a copy for each family member to keep. It helps if each of you has everyone's telephone number in one place. It also helps to have everyone's agreement on how decisions affecting your parent will be made.

This form included on the disk in the back of this book.

This agreement is good reminder to have in case one of your family members thinks they're too busy with say, a new job, a promotion, or a new baby when it comes time to help out with your parent. Everyone can find excuses when they don't want to do something, but helping a parent is something they should want to do. Use this opportunity to create a better relationship with your family as well as with your parent. Work out a way you can all participate, without putting undo pressure on anyone. There's always a way. Working together will strengthen your bond and bring you closer as a family. Isn't that what life is all about? Enlist your family today! Someday they may thank you for it. They will always respect you for it.

> "Use this opportunity to create a better relationship with your siblings as well as with your parent."

Early on, denial is often a key word. You, your family, and your parent can all deny there's anything wrong. If you all ignore the early warning signals, don't worry. There'll be plenty more signals to come. But start to act as soon as possible – before the fire engines and ambulances shock you into reality. Get your family together and have a heart-to-heart talk. Give them the current "state of the health" speech on your parent. Tell them what you've noticed about your parent's behavior. Then get everyone thinking about the future. Check into whether or not your parent has:

1. a will
2. a trust
3. a life directive
4. a death directive

5. preparation for future housing
6. long-term health care insurance
7. an insurance plan to pay funeral expenses

Each of you should know which of these they have and where they are kept.

We'll get into trusts, wills, and directives in Chapter 3. Use the list shown in Figure 1-3 to write down the names, addresses, and phone numbers of your parent's health care professionals in preparation for the next step – the doctor visit. Right now you need to get the communication lines open and flowing all both directions.

This form included on the disk in the back of this book.

If you get stuck at this stage and can't seem to move because your parent won't admit they need your help, or because you're at odds with an uncooperative family member, you're probably in the majority. Let me offer something you might try.

Family Enlistment Form

We, the undersigned agree to help in the care of our parent _____ We agree we will do our best to assist each other and our parent in all situations. We will call upon each other for emotional support, financial help, and physical help, within reason.

We agree to each take part in key decisions involving our parent's care, either by telephone, or if possible, in person. If we are not unanimously decided on what course of action to take regarding our parent's health or maintenance care, we will each have a vote in the decision and the majority will prevail. We agree to abide by and help put into effect the majority decision. If a decision is tied we will re-vote until a majority is represented.

Name_____ Date _____ Phone _____

Name_____ Date _____ Phone _____

Name_____ Date _____ Phone _____

Name_____ Date _____ Phone _____

Name_____ Date _____ Phone _____

Name_____ Date _____ Phone _____

Name_____ Date _____ Phone _____

Name_____ Date _____ Phone _____

Figure 1-2 Family Enlistment Form

Parent's Doctors

Doctor _____ Clinic _____

Specialty _____

Phone _____ Address _____

Doctor _____ Clinic _____

Specialty _____

Phone _____ Address _____

Dentist _____ Clinic _____

Phone _____ Address _____

Ophthalmologist_____ Clinic _____

Phone _____ Address _____

Other_____ Clinic _____

Specialty _____

Phone _____ Address _____

Figure 1-3 Parent's Doctors

First and foremost, forgive the person giving you grief in your heart and soul. Picture them in your mind and say to yourself that you forgive them. Let go of any hatred or ill feelings you've harbored against them. Picture them again in your mind and tell yourself that you really want to help them. If you are religious, ask for God's help to give you a hand. It never hurts to ask, and you may be surprised to find it works, maybe not always in the way you expect, but sometimes in an way you don't expect.

Notes

_____

_____

_____

_____

_____

_____

_____

_____

_____

_____

_____

_____

_____

_____

_____

_____

_____

_____

_____

_____

_____

_____

_____

_____

_____

_____

_____

CHAPTER 2

The Doctor Visit

The development or worsening of a health problem can quickly become a turning point in your parent's life. You may have had suspicions that something was wrong, or that something in their physical make-up had changed, but you were afraid to pursue the subject. Then one day, you just knew.

"We decided to take a little walk and she began huffing and puffing after we had gone only about 50 feet."

I remember when I first noticed my mother had a chronic health problem. We decided to take a little walk and she began huffing and puffing after we had gone only about 50 feet. When I mentioned it, she just said something like "Well, I'm not a young chicken any more." But I was really shocked. We had to turn back – and this just wasn't normal. My mom played basketball in college and always kept very fit. She included long walks in her exercise regimen, and continued walking and exercising as part of her routine after she retired. I knew something was wrong, but she wouldn't admit to it. She figured it was a natural part of the aging process. But it wasn't. I learned much later, after many tests and several doctors, that she had developed congestive heart failure. I wish now that I had done something about her condition sooner. It might have prolonged her life – or at least improved the quality of her life.

I'm not suggesting you become so vigilant that you check your parent's blood pressure every day. I'm just trying to tell you to act quickly on problems when they become apparent to you – especially chronic problems. If you've noticed any of the health changes we've discussed in the previous chapter, you need to become involved as soon as possible. It's important to make sure your parent sees a doctor. If you don't, the situation will only get worse.

My sister was the one who first took our mother to a doctor. And she continued to act on her own until she finally needed to enlist my help. Of course, there were demands on my time – my young son for one. And if I took off during the day, I would have to work late at the office to make up for the time I was away. But there were demands on my sister's time as well. So we started splitting up the doctor visits, and it worked out well for both of us. For me, each trip to the doctor became a special time with my mom. We had time alone together to just talk. We'd recant old stories, or exchange views of what we thought of the doctor or his staff, or whatever else might be happening in our lives. Looking back, I'm really glad I took those afternoons off. If I hadn't, I'd regret it now. Regular doctor visits were important in tracking her continuing health problems – and she simply wouldn't have gone on her own. Those were also important opportunities for us to become closer and more involved in each other's lives.

At first, my mother's doctor visits didn't seem to be getting us anywhere. She had been going to the same doctor for a number of years and he just continued to renew her prescriptions and give her a clean bill of health. When my sister and I started going with her, the doctor seemed reluctant to tell us exactly what was happening to Mom. He didn't have any answers for our questions. We managed to get a prescription to reduce the swelling in Mom's legs, but got no explanation as to what was causing the swelling, why she was short of breath, or why her memory seemed to be going. We decided it was time to change doctors.

> "One thing became very clear to us. You have to be your parent's advocate if you want them to receive good health care."

We ended up changing doctors six times. Several of the doctors we took our mother to were very nice people, but they failed to identify what was wrong or give us any idea of what we could do to help her. Mom probably got treated the way most older people get treated in doctors' offices across this country – everyone was very nice, but not very helpful. One thing became very clear to us. You have to be your parent's advocate if you want them to receive good health care. Hopefully, with the information that follows, you won't have to go through what we did to get help for your parent.

Evaluating Your Parent's Current Health Care

Before making that first doctor visit with your parent, take some time to sit down and talk with them about their health and the care they've been getting from their current doctor. Find out when their symptoms developed, what their concerns are, and what less-obvious problems they've been experiencing that may or may not be related. Find out which doctors they've already been to and what the diagnosis was. Get each doctor's phone number. You can use the Parent's Doctors list in Chapter 1. Write everything down.

Next go to the medicine cabinet and make a list of all the medications your parent is taking, including the strength of the medication and prescribed dosage. Don't leave anything out – even aspirin. Use the prescription checklist in Figure 2-1 as an aid. Educate yourself about each drug and its uses by looking them up on the Internet at the Web sites listed on the next page or in the *Physician's Desk Reference* at your local library. Take a good look at the side effects and see if any of the reactions sound familiar.

This form included on the disk in the back of this book.

Prescription Drug List

Current prescription list for _____ Date _____

Drug name	Dosage	Frequency	For how long?
_____	_____	_____	_____
_____	_____	_____	_____
_____	_____	_____	_____
_____	_____	_____	_____
_____	_____	_____	_____
_____	_____	_____	_____
_____	_____	_____	_____
_____	_____	_____	_____
_____	_____	_____	_____
_____	_____	_____	_____
_____	_____	_____	_____
_____	_____	_____	_____

Figure 2-1 Prescription Drug List

Then, go to the kitchen and check for vitamins, health foods, and natural remedies your parent may be taking. There are people who take all kinds of over-the-counter health medications. Your parent may be one of them. A friend tells them about this or that, and they go shopping at the health food store and come home with a bag full of natural cures for everything from insomnia to constipation. Some of these are good – but some are not so good. If your parent takes too much of a drug, or in combination with other drugs, they may have problems. Most people don't bother to tell their doctor they're taking ginkgo biloba, large doses of vitamin B or C, or other over-the-counter preparations. They think they're just vitamins and natural herbs – nothing worth mentioning. But everything is worth mentioning. Write all these down as well, and check them out on the Internet, looking for possible side effects.

Prescription Drug Web Sites

There are many Web sites that cover prescription drugs. Sometimes you can do a search for a drug on a search engine and find an amazing amount of information on that drug. Here are a few Web sites I found to be particularly helpful. By the time you get this book there'll probably be many more.

www.drkoop.com — This is a great health Web site that reports new developments in health care and research. It also has a great lookup search engine that will seek out any known drug by name and list everything about it.

www.healthsquare.com/drugmain.htm – Health Square is a general health Web site. Their drug/medicine site will allow you to look up almost any drug. Drugs are listed alphabetically and each listing includes all the brand and generic names that the drug is sold under. The listing also includes uses and side effects for each drug.

www.worstpills.org – This site lists one doctor's view of the worst prescription drugs.

www.Rxlist.com – This site lists valuable information on prescription and herbal drugs.

Medications

If your parent is taking daily medications, as most people over age 70 are, make sure they actually take the medications daily, and in the proper dosage. All sorts of mistakes can occur with medications. Or, they may be taking a dosage that's no longer correct for their current condition. If their health has changed, and the prescribed dosage hasn't been checked lately, it may be incorrect for their current condition.

Nearly 80 percent of people over 70 years old take some form of medication for high blood pressure, diabetes, heart trouble, kidney problems, or any number of other ailments. You name it, and there's a pill for it. But if they forget to take that pill or take a pill twice, or in the wrong combination, all sorts of side effects can occur. They may become dizzy, nauseous, or even faint for no apparent reason, and the cause of the incident can be a mystery. But the results can be devastating. You may find your parent passed out when you come to visit. Or you'll get a surprise call from the emergency room after your parent was found aimlessly wandering the neighborhood. If you ask your parent, they may claim they took their regular dose of pills at the right time. But in the back of your mind, you may have your suspicions.

This happened to my mother. One morning we received an emergency call from the hospital. Apparently Mom had passed out and hit something on the way down and cut herself. The cleaning lady found her unconscious and bleeding in her room. She was rushed to the hospital, kept for observation, and then released several days later. We never really knew what happened. My sister and I thought that she might have taken a double dose of her blood pressure pills. After this episode, we arranged to have someone give her the pills every morning. That seemed to work.

Medication Dispensers

As a person gets older and their memory begins to fade, they can easily forget which pills they took. You don't even have to be old to have this happen! Anyone who's on more than one type of medication can get confused about what they have, and haven't taken. Especially when there's five different bottles to take from every morning. Buy your parent one of those medicine containers that have a compartment for each day of the week, divided into AM and PM doses. You can put their medications in the container for the upcoming week and all your parent has to do is figure out what day of the week it is and open the compartment for that day. Have a calendar next to the container to make this easy for them. Check twice a week for a while to make sure they're getting the hang of it. If they can't, you'll probably have to hire someone to dispense the medicines every day, unless you can do it yourself.

Keep Your Perspective

If you haven't seen your parent in some time, keep in mind that the stress of everyday life can make dealing with simple things more challenging as your parent ages. There are bound to be some signs of mental and physical decline that are normal and not related to drug interaction or pathological problems. Don't become alarmed and rush to classify any medical problem right off the bat. Nothing is worse than an amateur diagnosis.

The little glitches in your parent's memory don't necessarily mean they have Alzheimer's or some form of dementia. These ailments are diagnosed in only 7 percent of people over age 65 and 20 percent over 80. At this stage your parent may be in normal health for their age. They may have a minor health problem that has become chronic because of lack of attention. They may need a change in a prescription for a drug they've been taking for the last 20 years. Or they may be lacking some vitamin or mineral, suffering from a minor infection, or just showing the natural symptoms of the aging process. But you won't know for sure until you get them evaluated by a doctor.

Your parent may need your help to take care of these problems and make sure they get follow-up health care. As you may discover, older people don't always receive the same level of care that younger people do. They are often treated on a different, and what I feel is a substandard level, unless someone, such as a spouse or one of their children, is in there fighting for them. So, if you're ready to do a little work on your own, you can get prepared to ask the right questions when you see the doctor. You need to find out what's wrong with your parent. If it's something simple, what do you do to make sure the problem goes away and doesn't reoccur? If there's something more serious, what can you do for them? What's the outlook for a full recovery? Or, if there's no hope of recovery, how can you help your parent cope with what they have? Hopefully if you're insistent enough, you won't have to go to six different doctors, as we did, to get your questions answered. Maybe you'll be able to get your parent's doctor to level with you and explain their problems, tell you what treatments are available, and what the chances for recovery are. The key to getting answers is being persistent, organized, and asking the right questions.

"As you may discover, older people don't always receive the same level of care that younger people do. They are often treated on a different, and what I feel is a substandard level, unless someone, such as a spouse or one of their children, is in there fighting for them."

Include Your Family Members

Before you actually make an appointment with a doctor, get on the phone and call your family members. Tell them what you've seen and why you're concerned. Enlist their support. Utilize the Family Agreement from Chapter 1. If you haven't discussed this agreement with your family members and had them sign it, now is the time. You'll need it in the days ahead. Keep them informed of what you're doing and enlist one or more of them to come with you to the doctor's office. Plan on attending the doctor's appointment with your parent – even if you both have to take time off work. This time is crucial for your family. If you don't attend, your parent may not know what questions to ask, or remember what information the doctor gives them. It's better to bring along the troops, even if you fill up the examination room. And it delivers a message to the doctor that this person's health is important, and he'd better treat it as such.

You want your parent to have a complete physical. Be there when your parent calls for the appointment, or make the call yourself, so the appointment can include a conference with the doctor for you, your parent, and your family members. It will help tremendously to have at least one of your family members along. They'll spread the word to other family members so you won't be the lone crusader in your parent's cause. It'll also ensure that you both hear the same thing from the doctor, so there won't be confusion later about what was actually said in the doctor's office. If it's just you and your parent there, I can almost guarantee you won't hear the same thing. Some patients focus on the negative, and some on the positive – they rarely have the detachment to get the whole perspective. That's why it's good to have someone else along when you get a diagnosis.

Getting Background Information for the Doctor

For this doctor visit, bring a current list of your parent's medications like the Prescription Drug List shown in Figure 2-1. You might also want to bring your notes on the information you found on the various medications. This will help you discuss your parent's need for the different medications. What they are for? What do they do? What are the possible side effects or drug interactions? You'll have some information, and the doctor can fill you in on the rest. If any of the known side effects match the symptoms your parent has, be ready to discuss them with the doctor. Write everything down so you'll have it in front of you when you're in the office.

> "You can learn all kinds of information from the prescriptions your parent is taking. Write down your questions so you can quiz the doctor."

By studying these medications you'll probably uncover a few things about your parent's health that you weren't aware of. You may be able to piece together a better medical history than your parent can tell you. You may even uncover some problems or complications that have been aggravated by the drugs they've been taking. For example, they may be continuing with a high blood pressure medication that was prescribed in the 1970s and has since been found to cause serious side effects in older people. Or, maybe they're taking a diuretic to alleviate swelling in their legs. But the swelling may be a symptom of a more serious problem that has never been diagnosed, such as failing kidneys or inability of their heart to pump blood properly. You can learn all kinds of information from the prescriptions your parent is taking. Write down your questions so you can quiz the doctor.

A few of the drugs commonly prescribed for older people may be some that have been reported as potentially dangerous. Be sure to bring these to the doctor's attention if your parent takes them. The doctor may pooh-pooh the bad press on these drugs, or he may take the time to explain to you why some doctors believe a drug is dangerous while others continue to prescribe it. Most doctors have their own opinion of drugs. If your parent is taking one of these drugs, ask the doctor why he prescribed that particular drug and if there's an alternative available that might work just as well.

Worst Drugs According to WWW.Worstdrugs.com

Atarax/Benadryl/Vistaril	Elavil	NSAIDs
Compazine	Iron Supplements	Quinidine/Procainamide
Dalmane/Klonopin/Valium	Haldol/Mellaril/Serentil	Reglan
Diabinese	Inderal	Verapmil
Digoxin	Lasix	

Organize Your Questions

This form included on the disk in the back of this book.

Write down all of the reasons you're there to see the doctor. Fill out the Symptoms Observed and Questions for the Doctor form shown in Figure 2-2 and make a list of everything you've noticed that concerns you. Have your questions ready to ask - even if your parent isn't anxious to participate in this discussion. This is an area where you need to take control. The future of your parent's health depends on it.

You should also get a family history of illnesses and cause of death for each of your parent's immediate family. This will prove helpful for you and your children as well. The Family Medical History form shown in Figure 2-3 will help you organize the information.

Use the checklist shown in Figure 2-4 to help you organize all the items and information you need to take with you when you go to see the doctor.

The Doctor

Even though you may think your personal doctor is the best doctor in the world, it's probably best to make this first visit with your parent's doctor. Your parent's doctor is familiar with your parent's problems, and just as important, your parent is familiar with their doctor. That familiarity can make the process of a physical examination a friendlier, less-threatening evaluation. You can always take your parent to your own doctor later, for a second opinion, if you feel it's necessary.

If your parent makes the appointment, call the doctor yourself, explain your concerns and advise him that you'll want to discuss your parent's condition and care. While you're on the phone, make sure the doctor accepts assignment from Medicare. This means the doctor won't charge your parent fees over what Medicare will pay. In other words, you want to make sure ahead of time that the exam will be completely covered by Medicare. Some older people carry a supplemental insurance policy that will pay the difference between what Medicare pays and what the doctor charges.

Symptoms Observed and Questions for the Doctor

Patient_____ Appointment date_____

Social Security #_____

Symptoms noticed:

1)_____

_____

2)_____

_____

3)_____

_____

Questions for the doctor:

1)_____

2)_____

3)_____

4)_____

5)_____

6)_____

7)_____

8)_____

9)_____

10)_____

Figure 2-2 Symptoms Observed and Questions for the Doctor

Family Medical History

Patient's name_____

Social Security number _____

Name of patient's mother _____

Mother's illnesses or cause of death _____

Other illnesses or physical/mental health symptoms _____

Name of patient's father _____

Father's illnesses or cause of death _____

Other illnesses or physical/mental health symptoms _____

Brother/sister's name _____

Brother/sister's illnesses or cause of death _____

Other illnesses or physical/mental health symptoms _____

Brother/sister's name _____

Brother/sister's illnesses or cause of death_____

Other illnesses or physical/mental health symptoms _____

Brother/sister's name _____

Brother/sister's illnesses or cause of death_____

Other illnesses or physical/mental health symptoms _____

Grandmother (mother's side) _____

Cause of death of grandmother _____

Other illnesses or physical/mental health symptoms _____

Grandfather (mother's side) _____

Cause of death of grandfather _____

Other illnesses or physical/mental health symptoms _____

Figure 2-3 Family Medical History

Checklist of Things to Bring to a Doctor Visit

❑ Health insurance records

❑ History of past illnesses and operations

❑ Symptoms and Questions form

❑ Prescription Drug List form

❑ List of over-the-counter drugs, herbal medications, and vitamins used

❑ Allergies

❑ Family medical history

❑ X-rays or tests (if possible)

Figure 2-4 Checklist of Things to Bring to a Doctor Visit

These people can consult any doctor they want to – because they have complete coverage. But most seniors depend on Medicare to cover their doctor's fees. Not every doctor will take assignment from Medicare, though I do know of cases where a doctor will agree to take assignment for a patient they've been seeing for many years. If your parent is covered by an HMO, find out if the doctor takes patients under that HMO plan before you make the appointment.

If the doctor is willing, discuss your concerns with him or fax him your Symptoms and Questions form before the appointment date so he can look into addressing the problems you've noticed with your parent. If the doctor already has the information on hand, it won't look like you're betraying any of your parent's confidences when you're at the actual visit. That way the doctor can ask your parent about possible problems, and you can all discuss what you've observed without appearing to initiate the discussion. Your parent will be less likely to go on the defensive if the doctor is the one bringing up the problems. Remember, you don't want to alienate your parent. You're the best friend they have – though they may not realize it yet.

During the appointment, let your parent take the lead, especially if the doctor has your form. Try to stay as quiet as possible, as the doctor may be checking your parent's responses. If the doctor is an old friend of your parent, he or she will put your parent at ease and make them comfortable throughout the examination.

If you've mentioned that your parent has been forgetful, the doctor may perform a field test memory exam. Be careful though, sometimes your parent can finesse the doctor. Don't let the doctor lose his impartiality. If the doctor determines your parent needs a psychiatric evaluation, he can recommend one. It usually requires a short stay at a geriatric assessment center in your community. We'll cover the details of this type of examination in Chapter 6. But before you head off for a geriatric evaluation, make sure you have all the legal documents we're going to go over in Chapter 3. If you don't, you'll have a lot of trouble getting these papers in order for the future.

Follow Up with the Doctor After the Exam

Usually the doctor will ask your parent questions about any symptoms, or their health in general, hopefully discussing what you noted in your checklist. Then he'll order some tests and some blood work and say he'll call you back in a few weeks with the results. Don't wait two weeks. Doctors are busy people and have lots of patients. Your parent may be just one more elderly person to them. Emphasize how important your parent's needs are to you, and that you want your parent started on a program to improve their health as soon as possible. Make a note on your calendar to call the doctor one week after your appointment. The doctor will probably be willing to talk with you by phone before you schedule a second exam. He may even ask you questions about what he sees as a result of the tests, or whether you've noticed any changes in your parent's behavior or condition.

"By calling the doctor, and not waiting for him to call you, you're showing that you want to get your parent's health issues resolved in a straightforward manner."

By calling the doctor and not waiting for him to call you, you're showing that you want to get your parent's health issues resolved promptly. Believe it or not, sometimes it's hard to get a straight answer from doctors. Show the doctor that you care and you're willing to explore anything that may help with managing your parent's health care. Let the doctor know that if you feel there's a problem to address, you're not going to go away until you get appropriate action from him. You'll also know you're doing all you can do for your parent at this stage, and that will help you sleep better at night.

Don't Take the Simple Answer - Get a Second Opinion

After you have a follow-up talk with the doctor, you'll have an idea about how you need to proceed. The doctor may tell you your parent is fine and you can stop worrying. There may be a simple explanation and remedy for your parent's problem. However, sometimes "fine" can mean that all is not "fine," but only that the doctor thinks your parent is elderly and has something for which there's no cure. Or maybe there is a cure, but he feels the cure may be more than your parent can take – like a heart, kidney, or liver transplant. Sometimes the doctor will say your parent is "fine" when your parent is acting downright crazy and you know for a fact they aren't "fine."

If the doctor doesn't recognize the problem, or says it's insignificant, get a second opinion right away. You'd be surprised at the number of people who have to do this. As I said earlier, we had to consult six doctors before we finally got a valid diagnosis for my mother's problems. Possibly the doctors were trying to let us down gently rather than hitting us over the head with the fact that Mom wouldn't get better. That, combined with our own denial of the problem, could have been one reason we had such a hard time getting the straight facts. In any case, we really had a difficult time finding out the truth about our mother's health – at least a truth that we, as folks not knowledgeable about health care, could understand, accept, and act on.

If you feel this is happening to you, get a second or third opinion from other doctors or from a geriatric specialist (a doctor who specializes in treating the elderly). Look up a medical referral agency in the yellow pages of your phone book and ask them for the phone numbers of gerontologists. These are physicians who have received specialized training in treating and managing the problems of older people. If you have a family and a heavy work

"Sometimes the doctor will say your parent is 'fine' when your parent is acting downright crazy and you know for a fact they aren't 'fine.'"

schedule, you may not have a lot of time to shop for doctors. But think about what's important here – closing a big deal for your boss, or taking the afternoon off to find a good doctor for your parent? It may be time to give your parent the best you can, just as they did for you. You might have to rethink your priorities and put a few things on hold. In the end, you'll be glad you did.

Accepting the Results

Sometimes the results from the doctor's exam aren't pleasant. But knowing the truth can help you plan the future and figure out what kind of action to take. The truth can help you overcome the demons of denial and inertia. Most of the time the doctor will have some simple recommendations to start with. He may change your parent's prescriptions, and recommend new medications. He may recommend potassium or iron supplements. He may recommend further tests. Sometimes, however, the doctor may find things that will require immediate changes in your parent's life, such as moving out of their present home and into a place where they can get 24-hour care.

Programs Available to Help Seniors

There's a lot of help out there for seniors. Don't think you're totally on your own when it comes to caring for your parent. If your parent can still live on their own and just needs help with meals, they can get meals delivered by Meals-on-Wheels. The meals may not be gourmet, but you can at least be sure your parent has a hot, nutritious meal every day.

If the doctor says your parent needs exercise or social interaction and should get out of the house more often than you can manage, there are senior programs designed just for that purpose. You can find them in the phone book or posted at the senior center in your area. There are many services available now for older people, often staffed by volunteers. Some will even come and pick seniors up if they don't have transportation. There are social and recreational activities to help seniors stay mentally and physically fit, exercise programs and physical therapy, counseling and group activities to help seniors cope with problems. Some of these are part of community services, some are services covered by Medicaid or state aid, some require a small contribution, and some have to be recommended by a doctor.

If your parent needs special care or on-going home care, the doctor may advise you to look into, and take advantage of, the social services available in your area. If your doctor doesn't bring this up, ask about them yourself. Sometimes doctors don't know what social programs your parent is eligible for. If that's the case, you may want to look into finding a geriatric care manager. You can find a list of geriatric care managers on the Internet at www.caremanager.org. Care managers charge from $60 to $200 per hour, but can be worth their weight in gold when referring you to help and setting up an action plan. They may be able to recommend programs in your area that can enhance your parent's quality of life and make their remaining years more enjoyable.

Here are some of the programs that may be available in your community:

● **Adult Day Health Care**: This is a Godsend for people who are physically or mentally frail. It usually offers a wide range of therapeutic, rehabilitative, and support activities, including nursing, assistance with life activities, social work services, meals, and sometimes even transportation. This service is available several hours a day (but not all day), usually during weekdays.

● **Companionship Services**: Companions are available to visit isolated or home-bound individuals for conversation, reading, letter writing, and light errands. Sometimes volunteers from a church provide these services.

● **Escort Services for the Elderly**: These services provide personalized escorts as well as personal assistance with shopping, doctor's visits, outings, and companionship.

> "You can find a list of geriatric care managers on the Internet at www.caremanager.org"

- **Home Delivered Meals:** There are nutritional programs, such as Meals-on-Wheels, that offer home delivered meals to seniors. Subsidized programs ask for voluntary contributions, while others may require full payment for delivery of a hot, well-balanced meal.

- **Home Health Aides:** These aides provide home health service as well as assistance with eating, dressing, hygiene, bathing, administering medications, and light household tasks. If a doctor orders this service, the costs may be covered by state health aid or Medicare.

- **Home Health Care:** There are organized programs that include social work, occupational therapy, physical therapy, and other rehab services to individuals in their home.

- **Homemaker Services:** These people provide help with shopping, laundry, light cleaning, dressing, preparation of meals, and escorting your parent to the doctor. You can obtain homemaker help through in-home health care agencies, the Area Agency on Aging, the Department of Social Services, and religious groups and organizations.

- **Housekeeping Services:** These are volunteer groups who help with cleaning, shopping, laundry, and meal preparation. Usually they charge a small fee, unless they're volunteers from a church.

- **Housing Assistance:** These programs help seniors find housing, such as shared housing or emergency shelters. The cost of the housing is usually paid by local government sources.

- **Physical or Occupational Therapy:** These are programs initiated by your doctor to build up the skills your parent needs for daily living. They may be paid in part by Medicare - depending on the circumstances.

- **Respite Care Services:** If you're caring for your parent by yourself, and are at your wits' end, these programs offer temporary relief for primary caregivers.

- **Speech Therapy:** You can get help for your parent if they have difficulty speaking, communicating, or swallowing as a result of stroke or other illness. If the doctor recommends a speech therapist, Medicare usually covers the cost.

- **Social Day Care:** This is like adult day care, but the activities are recreational and emphasis is on social skills. Usually transportation is provided.

- **Telephone Reassurance:** This is a volunteer organization that offers telephone contact and socialization to older people who are home alone. They may call every day or a couple of days a week just to make contact and provide assurance.

- **Transportation Services:** Many transportation services, such as Dial-a-Ride, Red Cross Wheels, Cancer Society, and Lifeline are available for a small fee.

The key here is that once you notice a problem with your parent, you have to wake up and take quick action. Older people can become complacent and resist any new action that takes them into areas of health care. With complacency comes the danger of decline and with older people that decline can be swift. It's up to you to get things done, because they probably won't get done without your help. Getting your parent to the doctor for a evaluation of their health is one of the first steps in your involvement in their life.

If you encounter resistance here, don't give up. Remind yourself that you're doing this to help your parent and not yourself. If you can't convince your parent that a doctor appointment is needed, even when to you the signs of need appear obvious, try using peer pressure. Have a friend or relative show up to back your cause. Hopefully your parent will give in and realize they need to let you take them to the doctor.

If everything fails – your parent is suffering and refuses help, and you can't enlist the help of a peer or other family member to help you, try turning to a higher source. I realize this may sound simplistic, but it worked for me. It may work when you're out totally of options with a loved one. Sometimes it's the only thing that does. Sometimes a simple prayer can work wonders.

CHAPTER 3

Signing Up for the Future

You've stirred up the anthill, and now you have to take action on what you've started. You need to get your parent's legal papers in order so you can protect their future and control some of the events heading their way. You may think it's a bit premature to sit down with your parent and talk about granting you power of attorney or setting up a trust; living will, and will. These aren't easy things to discuss. Funeral/memorial services and burial requests are even more difficult subjects. But if you don't talk about it soon, you may miss the opportunity.

Asking your parent to give you, or someone in your family, power of attorney over their affairs (both financial and health) might surprise or even anger them. They may not be ready for it – you may not be ready for it. But it's important that you take care of this as soon as possible. It must be done while your parent is competent and capable of making informed decisions. A good way to begin is to have a heart-to-heart talk with your parent. Tell them why they need to visit a lawyer and get some particular forms filled out and signed. You might want to include your family members in this discussion. There's power in numbers, and your parent may be more easily persuaded if everyone shows the same concern, or believes strongly that this is important. Make sure your family members understand why you need to do this so they can back you up if your parent puts up an argument. Have them read this chapter, visit some Web sites, and know the facts before you approach your parent.

Sometimes it helps to call or visit your local senior center and talk to someone who is close to your parent's age. Probably 65 percent of people attending senior centers have made out a trust and taken care of the legal arrangements needed for their continuing care. You might ask one of the seniors there to talk with your parent about the importance of getting all their legal papers in order. Your parent may

"Your parent may value the opinions of other seniors over yours – and it never hurts your case to add a little peer pressure. You know peer pressure works – it's worked on all of us from time to time."

value the opinions of other seniors over yours – and it never hurts your case to add a little peer pressure. You know peer pressure works – it's worked on all of us from time to time.

Whatever you do, don't give up. Continue talking to your parent and explaining why it's so important for them to do this. It may take some time – but it's for their own benefit. It's imperative that your family has a notarized power of attorney safely tucked away and ready to use when it's needed.

My sister was the first to bring up the subject of Power of Attorney for Health Care and Durable Power of Attorney to our mom. My brother-in-law suggested that she get it taken care of right away. Neither of us understood the true significance of having our mother sign the papers at that time. We didn't know how important it was going to be in caring for her future needs – or how soon we'd need them. We bought generic copies of the forms from a stationery store, and just assumed she would sign. However, when Mom questioned us about whether they were really necessary, we hesitated and didn't push the subject. We didn't have a good explanation ready for her, and she simply didn't want to sign. It took my sister and I six months to get her comfortable with the idea. By that time, Mom was starting to show obvious signs of dementia and we had to have a Notary Public come to the board-and-care where she was living to notarize the papers when she signed them. My sister and I were both worried and prayed silently that the Notary wouldn't notice that our mother was not entirely of sound mind. We just managed to squeak through this process. That's why I encourage you to do it as soon as possible - you just never know what's going to happen to change your parent's health.

It was only a short time before we realized the importance of having these forms available. Our mother was admitted to the hospital for an emergency operation and we needed a signed Power of Attorney for Health Care to make decisions on her care. While she was hospitalized, we also found out that Mom had set up a new bank account outside of her trust and had directed that her pension payments be sent to this account. It took our Power of Attorney to unravel this mess so we could continue to pay her bills while she recovered from surgery. We were thankful that Mom finally agreed to sign the forms and they were notarized and ready to use when we needed them.

> "It's imperative that your family has a notarized power of attorney safely tucked away and ready to use when it's needed."

Trusts

If your parent has assets of over $100,000 or real property, such as a house or land worth $20,000 or more, they may want to think about setting up a trust. Otherwise, when they die, all their assets may have to go through probate. A trust is an alternative to the probate process that will save the estate (and you) a considerable amount of money in court fees, legal costs, and taxes. A trust also takes less time to settle and allows you (if you are an appointed trustee or executor) to maintain control of your parent's assets.

Probate is a legal process in which the named executor (usually a family member who has to hire a lawyer) goes before a court and identifies and catalogs all of your parent's property, has the property appraised, pays all debts and taxes, proves that your parent's will is legally valid, and then distributes the property to you and the other heirs in accordance with the instructions in the will. This process can take up to six months and may involve thousands of dollars in legal fees. If your parent owns land in another state, you'll need to go through a separate probate in that state. The probate process is also part of the public record, which means that everyone will know your business and every phone solicitor will get you on their list.

During the probate period all of your parent's assets, including their checking account and savings, are in the hands of the executor. This person pays the bills, mortgage payment due on your parent's house, doctor and hospital bills, burial costs, and all the lawyer fees until the probate process is complete.

Setting Up a Trust

I recommend seeing a lawyer who can set up a Living Trust, a Power of Attorney for both Durable and Health Care, and a will, at the same time. Going through a lawyer usually assures that everything is done properly. Every state has its own rules and guidelines. An attorney will know the laws in your state and can draw up all the papers quickly and accurately. There are lawyers who specialize in trusts advertised in the newspaper, but they may not be the best ones for your needs. Usually word-of-mouth recommendations are best. If you don't know anyone who can recommend someone, check with your local senior center. You'll probably find someone who knows a good lawyer who enjoys working with older people. These lawyers usually know more about setting up trusts and asset protection for seniors than someone who deals in corporate or criminal law, and just does trusts as a sideline.

Don't Put Off Important Decisions

If you put off getting legal forms signed and helping your parent set up a will or trust, you may regret it later. Take your parent to see a lawyer and have everything taken care of at one time. These are the basic forms you need:

● **Power of Attorney for Health Care:** This form names the person responsible for making health care decisions and carrying out the Life Directives as written.

● **Life Directive – Living Will:** This is a plan, set up by your parent, with instructions on how they want to be cared for should they become incapacitated or rendered incompetent to make decisions regarding their health care. It usually includes a clause which states that they do, or do not, wish to be kept alive by artificial methods should the doctors determine that they have no chance of recovery. It may also include their wish to make anatomical gifts.

● **Death Directive:** A plan, set up by your parent, which states their preference regarding the disposal of their remains once they have passed on. It should say whether they want a conventional burial, cremation, or if they want to donate their body to science. They may also include the type of funeral or memorial service they prefer, and provide details of how they want their wishes carried out by the family.

● **Trust/and or Will:** Each state has their own limit, but as a rule-of-thumb, if your parent has liquid assets of over $100,000 or any real property, they

(continued on next page)

Don't Put Off Important Decisions (continued)

should establish a trust and name someone reliable as the executor of the trust (it can be friend or an attorney). A comprehensive trust can include Advance Directives and Power of Attorney. If your parent doesn't need a trust, they should have a Will drawn up which states how they want their property distributed and names an executor to carry out their wishes.

Some states, such as California, may have laws that combine Medical Power of Attorney and a Living Will into one document called an Advance Health Care Directive.

There are also lawyer referral services set up through the local bar association that can help you find an attorney that specializes in this area. If you have an accountant or family attorney, you can ask them for referrals as well.

Unfortunately, a lawyer will charge anywhere from $300 to $2,800 or more to set up a trust, depending on the assets involved. This may seem expensive, but if your parent has considerable assets, a Living Trust can ensure the future of both you and your parent. Most people pay a lawyer to set up their trusts, just like most people pay a mechanic to take care of their car. And like a car, a trust needs occasional maintenance. You can do it yourself, if you have the time. But most of us don't have the time or energy to keep up with current tax laws, and to make sure we've done all the proper things such as appoint a proper successor trustee, or correctly fund the trust. Trust lawyers I've spoken to claim that the largest problems they face are trusts that are improperly set up or poorly maintained. Sometimes it pays to call in a professional trust lawyer and have a trust done right.

If you're completely against lawyers or your parent thinks a lawyer is just too costly, there's an excellent book put out by Nolo Publishing called *Make Your Own Living Trust* that's available for less than $40. Although written by a lawyer, it's easy to read and understand, and contains the essential forms you'll need to make a legal trust. You can order it using the order form I've included in the back of this book.

My mother always tried to keep her financial affairs in good order. She had a trust drawn up long before we knew about it. The only problem was that she had it done by a lawyer she found in one of those little ads in the newspaper. It didn't cost her much, but her most important asset, a small piece of property, was never placed in the trust. When Mom died, my sister and I had access to her assets – all except for that parcel of land. It cost us about 25 percent of the appraised value of the land to get it transferred into our names.

Types of Trusts

There are many types of trusts for different needs. The most common trust, and the most simple to set up, is a Living Trust. A Living Trust created during the lifetime of your parent usually becomes irrevocable when your parent dies. Most of their assets, such as bank accounts, stocks, land holdings, houses, their business, and personal items of value, are usually placed in the trust. Property deeds are retitled and reregistered, and bank and savings accounts are renamed in the name of the trust. Assets must stay in the trust where they are protected from probate, and new assets must be added into the trust.

When the trust is established, your parent must designate a successor to serve as a trustee or executor. This should be a trusted individual your parent can rely on to get things done without delay, whose only agenda is to carry out your parent's wishes. A trustee or executor can, for example, write checks on your parent's bank accounts when necessary to pay their house payments, doctor bills, or buy groceries for them when they can't. (You can also accomplish this by simply opening a joint bank account if your parent doesn't need a trust.) The trust becomes a third party entity for managing your parent's assets. When your parent dies, you have no need for probate because all of your parent's assets and property were listed, categorized, and appraised when the trust was set up. But property may have to be re-appraised if estate tax or the value of the property affects distribution. The contents of the trust are then distributed according to the will that's included as part of the trust records.

Living trusts are usually revocable and changeable as long as your parent is alive. There are also revocable and irrevocable living trusts. An irrevocable trust can't be changed once your parent sets it up.

Specialized Trusts

There are also different types of specialized trusts that may be applicable for your needs:

Marital and Bypass Trusts (also known as A/B Trusts). These are trusts used to reduce or eliminate federal estate taxes owed by a husband and wife. Under current estate tax law, a marital trust can shield up to $1,350,000 from federal taxes, verses the $675,000 you'd be able to shield as a one-time tax shelter without a trust. An A/B Trust is a way for a couple to avoid paying taxes on any part of the property on an estate worth over $675,000. In setting up an A/B Trust you almost always set up a single Initial Trust that is revocable. This Initial Trust ends at the death of either partner and is split into two new trusts (A and B). This split takes place because of a paragraph in the Initial Trust stating that upon the first death, the A and B Trusts are to be created. Upon this death, the trustee (usually the surviving spouse) divides the property from the Initial Trust and places some of the property into the A and the B Trust. B in this case, usually stands for "below the ground." The B trust usually pays income to the survivor and passes the principal to children and grandchildren. The tax goal of the B trust is to get this money out of the couple's combined estate so it escapes estate taxation after the second spouse's death. If this sounds complicated it's because it is. If your parents have more than $675,000 in assets or real property, have them ask their lawyer about an A/B Trust.

Special-Needs Trusts. This trust is used to set up assets for a relative, such as a disabled child, who is unable to care for his or her needs and is receiving public assistance. Typically, a trustee is appointed to manage the assets for the relative.

Qualified Terminable Interest Property (QTIP) Trusts. This is like an A/B Trust, except the surviving spouse cannot change the portion of the estate directed to the children. This type of trust is often used to guarantee an income to a surviving spouse, but still pass the estate on to the children of a previous marriage. The QTIP trust provides for the spouse, but when he/she dies, the children receive the remaining assets as directed by the first spouse.

Charitable Remainder Trusts. This is an irrevocable trust that allows a person to direct some or all of their assets to a charity. Sometimes they will receive income from the trust until they die, then all the remaining assets go to the charity. They can also have the assets go to their children or other heirs. When the heirs die, the remaining assets go to the charity. With this type of trust, some or all of the assets eventually end up going to the charity.

Irrevocable Life Insurance Trusts. This trust protects the death payment in life insurance policies from estate taxes. The life insurance is placed in an irrevocable trust and the owner of the policy names his/her heirs as the beneficiaries. When the insured dies, the death payment remains in the trust where the beneficiaries can draw from it tax free. In an Irrevocable Life Insurance Trust it's important for the trustee to be independent from the family, and the monthly payments for the insurance come from a source other than the insured.

> "A trust is probably your parent's best first step in asset protection. For more involved asset protection, have your parent check with their trust lawyer."

A trust is probably your parent's best first step in asset protection. For more involved asset protection, have your parent check with their trust lawyer. Give them a list of questions that pertain to the subject of their assets, and ask them to have the lawyer recommend a reliable financial planner. Usually a lawyer who deals in asset protection will work with one or more financial planners, and will be able to give them a few referrals. I'll discuss this in more detail in Chapter 7.

Who Needs A Trust

If your parent has real property, a business, or sizable assets, they should definitely consider a living trust. Here are a few more reasons they might want to have a trust:

• To avoid probate in another state. If your parent owns property in more than one state, you'll need to hire a probate lawyer and pay court fees for each state.

• Confidentiality. With a living trust there is no public record of the proceeding. Even if you don't expect television reporters to show up at your parent's probate hearing, you may still want to keep your affairs private. All probate hearings are part of the public record.

- If you anticipate that your parent may not be capable of managing their finances in the future. They need to assign a successor trustee, which in some cases can be you or one of your family, who will manage the trust if a physical or mental illness prevents your parent from being able to do it. This protects them from unscrupulous relatives or friends who might try to exploit their illness and take their wealth.

- If your parent owns a business. Running a business is tough. Imagine trying to run a business that's tied up in court. Then try to imagine how difficult it would be to sell that business if you couldn't afford to keep it going through the probate process. Without a trust, your parent's business could spend a year in legal limbo while the court decides who should own it, how its debts should be paid, etc. How low can the value of the business go while you're waiting? You probably don't want to find out.

Who Doesn't Need a Trust

I know that today most families with property or assets have a Living Trust. It's almost a status symbol to have one. But not every family needs a trust. Why spend the money if you don't really need one? Here are a couple of reasons your parent might avoid setting up a trust:

> ## Once in a Trust, Always in a Trust
>
> Once your parent sets up a Living Trust, make sure they don't change banks. Sometimes, as people age, they become forgetful and open new accounts. They may even have their retirement checks direct-deposited into that new account, like my mother did. If the account at the new bank isn't set up as a trust account, you're not going to be able to get access to the money without a Power of Attorney. And while your parent may not need your help now, eventually you'll probably have to help them buy groceries or pay doctor bills using the money in their checking or savings account.
>
> Also, if they buy or inherit any additional land or real property after they've set up a trust, they must sign title to the property into the trust. Otherwise, the property will be outside the trust and you'll have to pay a lawyer and go through probate proceedings to get title to that property when they die – even though they had a trust. It's important that *everything* is in the name of the trust.

- As Bob Dylan once said in a song, "If you ain't got nothing, you ain't got nothing to lose." That phrase just might apply to your parent. Not everyone has a lot of assets. Probate fees are typically a percentage of the estate. If your parent's estate (all their material wealth) is less than $25,000, setting up a trust may not be worth the expense. It might cost more than you'd have to spend on probate. In many states, small estates are exempt from probate. In California, residents can leave up to $100,000 to their heirs without going through probate. If your parent doesn't own a home or any other real property and they don't have other large assets, you can just set up a joint bank account so you can pay their bills for them. When they die, the money in the account automatically goes to you. They can get along fine with just a simple will (but you still need the Power of Attorney).

- If your parent doesn't own property, but has money in life insurance policies, individual retirement accounts, and other contractual plans that already designate a beneficiary, they may not need a trust. Again, you just need a joint bank account, or power of attorney, so you can help pay their bills when they aren't able.

Sample for Health Care Power of Attorney

I appoint the person designated below to make health care decisions for me as allowed by the State of
_____ Civil Code. This power of attorney shall not be affected by my possible incapacity.

I, _____, do designate and hereby appoint

(Name)_____ (Address) _____ (City/State/Zip)_____

(Name)_____ (Address) _____ (City/State/Zip)_____ as my agent(s) to
make the health care decisions for me.

If I become incapable of giving consent with respect to health care decisions, I hereby grant the agent listed here full power
and authority to make health care decisions for me, for any type of care, treatment, service, or procedure to maintain, diagnose, or
treat a physical, or mental condition; to consult with and instruct my health care providers; to execute any documents necessary to
give, refuse, or withdraw permission, and to receive and release medical information consistent with my wishes stated below, and
my personal values and philosophy as known to the agent.

End-of-Life Decisions: In making decisions concerning life-sustaining treatment, my agent listed above is to consider relief of
suffering, and the probable future quality as well as the extent of the extension of my life. Should I have an incurable and irreversible condition, and if the extension of my life would result in mere biological existence, then I do not desire any life-sustaining
procedure of any form, including nutrition and hydration unless necessary for my comfort or the alleviation of pain; or if life-sustaining treatment has been instituted, then I desire that it be withdrawn.
Unless:_____(Add additional sheets if needed.)

Pain Relief: It is my desire that my agent consent and arrange the administration of any type of pain relief, even though its use
may lead to addiction, or even hasten the moment of, but not intentionally cause, my death, should I be diagnosed with an incurable or terminal condition or illness.

Alternate Agent: If my agent designated above is unable or unavailable to make health care decisions for me, I designate the
following person to serve in their place as my agent:

Alternate Agent: (Name)_____ (Address) _____
(City/State/Zip)_____

I understand that this power of attorney for health care will exist indefinitely unless I establish a shorter time. If I am not able to
make health care decisions for myself when this power of attorney expires, the authority I have granted my agent will continue to
exist until the time when I become able to make health care decisions for myself once again.

I sign my name to this Durable Power of Attorney for Health Care on _____ (Date)

Signature_____

(Name)_____ (Address) _____ (City/State/Zip)_____

On (Date)_____, before me, the undersigned, a Notary Public in and for the State of_____,
personally appeared (Name)_____ personally known to me or proved to me on the basis of satisfactory evidence to be the person whose name is subscribed to the within instrument and acknowledged that he executed it.

I declare under the penalty of perjury that the person whose name is subscribed to this instrument appears to be of sound
mind and under no duress, fraud, or undue influence.

WITNESS my hand and official seal._____

Figure 3-1 Sample for Health Care Power of Attorney

Power of Attorney for Health Care

If you go to a lawyer to have a trust set up, have a health care directive which can be a Power of Attorney for Health Care (sometimes called the Medical Power of Attorney) and Durable Power of Attorney set up at the same time. The lawyer will be able to customize the forms for your parent's needs and ensure that the forms meet the legal requirements of the state your parent resides in.

You can also purchase generic forms for Power of Attorney for Health Care at just about any stationery store. Each state has their own rules and their own specialized forms, so I can't supply a generic form in this book that you can use. I have included a sample form, shown in Figure 3-1, to help you identify what you'll need. Buy a form, fill it in, and have your parent sign it in front of a notary public. It's sometimes necessary to have witnesses at the signing as well. Have your parent keep the original, and keep a notarized copy for yourself. That way, if you ever get a call in the middle of the night advising you that your parent has been taken to the hospital, you'll have it handy. When it comes time to make life-and-death decisions about your parent's health care, you'll need to wear that form like a badge and hold it up like a shield. It will allow you to make choices for your parent when they can't make them for themselves.

Take care of this before your parent is unconscious in the emergency room or becomes mentally incapacitated. If you have family members who are close by and willing to help, see if your parent wants to have their names on it as well. Then, you can share the responsi-

"When it comes time to make life and death decisions about your parent's health care, you'll need to wear that form like a badge and hold it up like a shield."

bility for making important health decisions. The only problem with this is when you may have to agree on issues at short notice. Most lawyers will recommend that only one person in the family be the one to make the key decision, and they recommend this from experience. If your family is often divided on key issues, elect the most level-headed and responsible person as the one to sign these forms. Make sure your parent agrees with your recommendation.

Durable Power of Attorney for Finances

"All the Durable Power of Attorney means is that they have legally "deputized" you to care for their needs if they can't – which includes making out checks to pay bills and buy essentials, entering into contracts, buying, selling and renting out properties, and filing taxes."

This form names the person responsible to care for the legal and financial needs of your parent if, or when, they are incapacitated. This person is authorized to sign checks and documents, enter into contracts, and otherwise act as their legal agent.

Again, you can have a lawyer draw up a Durable Power of Attorney or you can buy the generic forms at a stationery store. This isn't an easy form for many parents to sign. They often feel like they're giving you power to take over their life. You can assure them that this isn't the case. All the Durable Power of Attorney means is that they have legally "deputized" you to care for their needs if they can't – which includes making out checks to pay bills and buy essentials, entering into contracts, buying, selling and renting out properties, and filing taxes.

Signing this power over to someone else is a leap of faith for most independent seniors. It was for my mother. And, like me, you may feel uncomfortable asking for Durable Power of Attorney over your parent's affairs. But when you need it, it's there. My sister and I were so glad we had that form available when we needed it! When my mother's health began to fail, we were able to step in, hold things together financially and take care of her. Again, and I can't overemphasize this, your parent must sign this *while they are competent to make such decisions.*

If You Don't Have a Durable Power of Attorney

If you don't get this document signed, and your parent has a stroke, or is declared incompetent by a doctor, you'll have to take your parent to court to have someone named as guardian. This can be a lengthy, expensive, and sometimes humiliating procedure. You don't want to put your parent through this if it can be avoided. It certainly isn't the way to build trust. Believe me, you don't want the last years of your parent's life to be spent resenting you for taking control away from them. Going to court for this is a lose-lose situation.

Sample Durable Power of Attorney

I, _____ the undersigned, hereby appoint as my true and lawful attorney for me and in my name, place and stead for my use and benefit:

Name_____ Address_____ City/State/Zip_____

as my agent (attorney-in-fact) to act for me in any lawful way with respect to the following subjects I have initialed and not to those that I have purposely not initialed:

_____ **To handle claims and litigation:** to recover, collect and receive money, debt, account, interest income, dividend, annuity, and demand belonging to me. I also give them the right to release debts or to settle debts to the best of their abilities and to handle and transact business in my name.

_____ **To handle real property transactions:** to contract for, purchase, receive, and take possession of and hold title to, and to lease such property for any term or purpose, including business, residence, or oil and mineral development. To sell, exchange, grant, or convey such property with or without warranty. To transfer in trust, or otherwise encumber if needed, to secure payment for any obligation or agreement.

_____ **To handle personal property transactions** ... buy, sell, exchange, transfer, and in any legal manner deal with mortgage, transfer in trust or otherwise ... ber the property to secure payment of a negotiable or non-negotiable note, or performance of any obligation or agreement.

_____ **Stock & bond transactions** to ... money and ... deliver negotiable or non-negotiable notes with or without security, and to loan money and receive negotiable or non-negotiable notes as security as deemed proper or necessary.

_____ **Estate, trust and other beneficiary transactions:** to create, change, supplement and terminate any trust and to instruct the trustee of any trust where I may be trustor, or beneficiary.

_____ **Business operating transactions:** to transact business as my act and sign, execute, acknowledge and deliver any business document as necessary.

_____ **Benefits from social security, medicare, civil or military service, or retirement plans**: to transact as necessary.

_____ **Tax matters:** to transact as necessary and honestly report in my absence and make payment for any due taxes.

Notice to Person Executing Durable Power of Attorney

By signing this document, you are enabling another person to act for you on important matters. However, you should consider the following:

1. Unless otherwise noted, this Durable Power of Attorney is effective immediately and will continue until it is revoked.

2. This document gives your appointed agent the right to act on your behalf, the duties noted above.

3. You can give special instructions to limit or extend the powers granted to your agent._____

_____

4. The powers you give to your appointed agent will last a lifetime, unless you state that the Durable Power of Attorney will exist for a shorter amount of time, or you terminate the Durable Power of Attorney. The Durable Power of Attorney will continue to exist even if you become incapacitated unless indicated here:_____

5. You can amend or change this Durable Power of Attorney by executing a new Durable Power of Attorney, or by executing an amendment to this Durable Power of Attorney. You have the right to revoke or terminate this Durable Power of Attorney at any time, as long as you are competent and of sound mind.

Figure 3-2 Sample Durable Power of Attorney

Sample Durable Power of Attorney (continued)

6. If I have appointed more than one agent, the agents are to act _____ (If you appoint more than one agent with Power of Attorney and you want each agent to act alone without the other agent joining, write "separately," otherwise write "jointly." If you write "jointly," all of your agents must act or sign together.

I agree that any third party who receives a copy of this document may act under it. Revocation of the Durable Power of Attorney is not effective as to a third party until the third party has seen or has actual knowledge of the revocation. By accepting or acting under the appointment, the agent(s) assumes the fiduciary and other legal responsibilities of an agent.

Witness this _____ day of _____, _____

State of _____ County _____

On _____ before me, _____

personally appeared _____

personally appeared _____

personally appeared _____

Witness my hand and official seal.

_____ (Seal)

I declare under penalty of perjury under the laws of the state of _____ that the person who signed this document is personally known (or proved to us on basis of convincing evidence) to be the principal who signed this Durable Power of Attorney in my presence. Name_____ Date_____

Figure 3-2 Sample Durable Power of Attorney (continued)

What Happens if a Parent Won't Sign the Papers

If you have some good heart-to-heart discussions with your parent about their future, and are patient, chances are pretty good they'll eventually sign the Durable Power of Attorney and Power of Attorney for Healthcare. However, if you don't get it done in time, and your parent is diagnosed with a deteriorating mental condition, the courts will have to step in. You'll have to hire a lawyer to file a petition with the court, and the court will interview specialists regarding your parent's competency. A lawyer will be assigned to represent your parent. If your parent is declared incompetent, the court will assign a legal guardian to control your parent's affairs. It's a time-consuming and emotionally draining experience – especially if your parent insists they are competent and decides to fight. It's best to do everything you can before conditions reach this point. No matter how many dinner discussions it takes, even if you have to fly in family members from another state to help you, it will be worth it in the long run.

Life Directives

Life directives are the instructions relating to health care that your parent wants you to follow should they become incompetent or incapable of making their final wishes known. They can be an independent document, or part of a Living Will. The Living Will, which is usually included as part of their trust, puts their wishes into a legal document. It typically mandates the manner in which your parent wishes to die, usually specifying that their death be pain-free, and limiting aggressive therapies to prolong their life if there is no chance for recovery. If the Living Will is the vehicle, the Medical Power of Attorney appoints the chauffeur and the directions to carry out the plan. It names the person or persons responsible for making sure these final wishes are carried out.

Living Wills are regulated by state requirements and have strict guidelines as to how they are to be handled, stored, and activated. The terms in these documents can be broad and sweeping and composed in complicated legal terms that offer few clear guidelines for ordinary people to grasp. Usually the lawyer setting them up takes the wording from a generic version stored on his computer. Help your parent define their wishes in clear terms before visiting a lawyer. Where do they want the cut-off point to be in their life? It'll be easier for you to carry out these decisions if you've discussed them with your parent. Use the Life Directive shown in Figure 3-3 and the Living Will shown in Figure 3-4 as guides to clarify what your parent wants, before visiting the lawyer. Have the lawyer draft these specific requests into the Living Will instead of using a generic form.

This form included on the disk in the back of this book.

Having a clear life directive from your parent makes it easier to carry out their wishes when the time comes. It also helps avoid arguments among family members, decreases feelings of guilt, and defines the appropriate actions you should follow at the final stage of your parent's life. It's important to have a detailed directive from your parent. There's no room for ambiguity. If, for example your parent doesn't want to be kept alive by artificial means, make sure they specify what "artificial means" they're referring to. Is it a respirator? Is it a heart pump? Is it a colostomy tube? Is it a feeding tube? What exactly do they mean?

Sometimes there's a need for someone to be kept alive by artificial means. They may have to be on a respirator following surgery, for example. Once on the respirator, if things go wrong, how long should they remain on the respirator? Have your parent specify when they want to be removed from artificial life support systems so that you won't have to be the one making the life or death decision.

Sample Life Directive

I _____ on this _____ day of _____ in the year _____, declare that it is not my wish to be kept alive by artificial means for a period of time exceeding ( ) 12 hours; ( ) 24 hours; ( ) 3 days; ( ) 1 week; ( ) 1 month; ( ) 6 months.

I define "artificial means" as:

( ) a machine respirator; ( ) a heart pump; ( ) a feeding tube; ( ) a colostomy tube;

( ) a hydration tube.

( ) I give the order to not resuscitate me should my heart fail.

Other: _____

_____

_____

I do ( ) I do not ( ) want to be an organ/tissue donor. As an organ donor, artificial support may be maintained long enough for the organs to be removed.

I give full responsibility to _____ or any of my children to enable this directive. By doing so they will be fulfilling one of my last requests.

Signed _____ Date_____

Figure 3-3 Sample Life Directive

My mother didn't want to be kept alive by artificial means, but unfortunately she needed an operation for diverticulitis. After this major operation, in which they removed a large part of her intestine, she was put on a respirator for 48 hours and a feeding tube was implanted in her stomach. She was fed *Ensure* via this feeding tube for months. Were we in violation of her request? Did we violate her directive by keeping her alive through artificial means? Probably. But we thought she had a chance of recovery. Not always a good chance – but a chance. Eventually she recovered, the feeding tube came out, and she was able to enjoy a few more precious months of life. You sometimes have to make the call on the finer points. How much is too much? It's never an easy call to make.

Directives give you guidelines your parent sets up and wants you to go by, but you're the one who has to enforce those wishes. Sometimes you have to use your own discretion in deciding how to interpret the guidelines. Leave some room for the unforeseen problem. Life isn't always as simple as what we write on a directive. The directives should be their choice. But they should be very clear and leave no room for ambiguity. Making choices like these for your parent is very difficult.

Sample Living Will

I want my doctors and my family to know that if I have a terminal condition, and there is no reasonable chance that I will recover no matter what treatment is provided, I wish aggressive medical treatment to be suspended. I want to die naturally. I want only medicines and treatments that will make me pain free. I want cleanliness, privacy, and peace in my last days.

If I cannot eat, I do ( ) I do not ( ) want a feeding tube placed in my veins, nose, throat, or surgically placed in my stomach to give me food and fluids to sustain my life beyond a reasonable time. I define a "reasonable time" as that which is necessary to determine if there is a likely possibility of my recovery.

I do ( ) I do not ( ) want to be an organ/tissue donor. As an organ donor, artificial support may be maintained long enough for any organs to be removed.

This Living Will is my choice and my decision. I fully accept the consequences of refusing medical treatment and medical care under the circumstances that I have named above. I realize that I can change my mind at any time; but if I do not choose to do so, it is my desire that my doctors and family honor this Living Will.

Signed _____ Date_____

Print name _____

Witness Statement: I believe the ad__t __e signed this Living Will i_ me__t__y competent, understands the purpose of the Living Will, and has signed it freely and without coercion. __ __ __ n__ __a__ly m__ __ber of the signer, and will not benefit financially from his/her death. I am not a doctor car___ fo__ __is pers__ n, __r __n__ __r __ __ployee of the doctor, or of any health care facility in which he/she is being treated or __re __ __.

Signed _____ Date_____

Print Name _____

Notary Statement:

I _____ a Notary Public of the state of _____

find the adult who signed this document to be mentally competent.

Witness this _____ day of _____, (witness)_____

State of _____Witness my hand and official seal.

_____ (Seal)
    (signature of Notary)

We declare under penalty of perjury under the laws of the state of _____ that the person who signed this document is personally known to us (or proved to us on basis of convincing evidence) to be the principal who signed this Living Will in our presence. Signed this _____ day of _____, (Name) _____ personally known to me (or proved to me on the basis of satisfactory evidence) to be the person(s) whose name(s) is/are mentioned in the living will as the person(s) executing Living Will and that his/her/their signature on this paper is that of the person executing the Living Will.

Signed _____ Date_____
              Witness

Print Name _____

Signed _____ Date_____
              Witness

Print Name _____

Figure 3-4 Sample Living Will

No one wants to play God. A good directive should make you feel like the decision was made by your parent and you're just helping carry it out.

If your parent doesn't need a trust, but you want an Advanced Directive that's officially recognized in your state, there's a non-profit organization called *Choice In Dying* that offers state-specific Advance Directives. You can contact them at 1-800-989-9455 or visit their Web site at www.choices.org. There's also a great software program on directives called *The Healthcare Directive (Living Will)* by Nolo Press (you can order it on the order form in the back of this book). This program explains all about health care directives and helps you set up and print out a comprehensive healthcare directive that's legal for your state.

Death Directives and Last Requests

What is going to happen to your parent when their life ends? Do they want to be cremated and their ashes scattered at sea or dropped from a plane over some special site? Do they want to be buried in the family plot in the Ozarks or next to a loved one? Or perhaps they want their body donated to science?

My mother never talked to us about death. My aunt told us, much to our surprise, that Mom wanted her ashes scattered in the bay at Monterey, California. So, we had a funeral service with friends and family and then, when the time was right, my sister and I went to Monterey. We rented a two-person kayak and paddled out beyond the swells. Although we had some rough surf and a few boats to contend with, our private service for our mother was carried out in a beautiful, but bittersweet way. It was very special and something that my sister and I will always remember.

Figure 3-5 is a sample Death Directive, which should give you clear instructions as to what, how, and where your parent would like their remains disposed of. You may not be able to fulfill all their requests due to

"When the time comes, you can plan a little ceremony with your family and do your best to carry out your parent's last request."

Death Directive

It is my last request that when I die, my body:

☐ be buried at _____

☐ be buried with my _____

☐ be cremated, and my ashes _____

☐ be donated to science (medical facility/university preferred)_____

☐ _____

At my funeral/memorial service I would like:

_____

_____

_____

I give full responsibility to _____ or my children to enable this directive. By doing so they will

be fulfilling one of my last requests.

Signed _____ Date_____

Witnessed by_____ Date_____

Figure 3-5 Death Directive

monetary and legal considerations. Not all states will let you throw your parent's ashes into the wind or drop them from a plane. But at least you'll have their request in writing. When the time comes, you can plan a little ceremony with your family and do your best to carry out one of your parent's last requests.

Preparing these directives and getting them signed is part of planning for your parent's future as well as the end of their life. This should be done with love and consideration for their feelings and their fears. Encourage your parent to talk with you about their fears. What do they fear most; losing their memory, a chronic painful condition, incontinence or loss of bodily control, loneliness, dying alone? The more they explore these fears and get them out in the open, the easier it will be for you to help your parent overcome them. Holding fear inside makes it grow – often way out of proportion. Talk with them as often as you can. If possible, based on their own religious preference, encourage them to feel that they're heading to a better place. It's important that you help them find peace with themselves. At least

This form included on the disk in the back of this book.

This form included on the disk in the back of this book.

let them know what an important significance they've had upon your life. It's a time for them to be introspective and to reflect on their life. It's not going to be easy for you either. Help share their burdens – provide them with as much physical and emotional comfort as you can by being there for them when they need you.

While you're having these discussions, it might be a good time to prepare an obituary fact sheet like the one in Figure 3-6. You don't have to use the word "obituary" if it seems morbid to you. Tell your parent you want to get all their "life" information together. Make it a positive experience – find out about all the peaks in their life – the best times, their favorite memories, how it felt to be honored by their peers, and what were the important events to them.

Right after your parent's death, while making arrangements and preparing for the funeral or memorial service, your emotions are strained and it's a real challenge to get all this information together, especially the dates. One of the nicest things you can do for your parent is to honor their life with a wonderful obituary published in their local newspaper. But that's very difficult to do when you can't remember the important events of their life and when they took place. Let your parent help you prepare this fact sheet while they're still alive. How I wish I had done this!

Reward Yourself

After everything is filled out, signed, notarized, and witnessed, make sure your parent stores the trust and the directives in a place where you can find them and access them in case of an accident. If your parent is forgetful, you may want to keep a copy for yourself.

Once you get all these legal papers taken care of, treat everyone to dinner. Make it a reward for putting up with the tensions and hassle of getting through the legal morass. This is one of the most difficult steps in your parent's care, because you have to push so much to complete the process. However, when you get over these legal hurdles, the rest of the steps covered in this book will fall into place and come about of their own accord. You'll have taken the steps you need to secure your parent's, and your own, future.

Give yourself a pat on the back – you deserve it. When my sister and I finished getting through all this paperwork, we went out for a great Mexican dinner with plenty of margaritas!

Personal Information Fact Sheet

Please use the following information for my obituary.

Personal data:

Name _____ Nickname_____

Birth date _____Birthplace _____

Moved to current location (date) _____from _____

Married to whom _____ Year _____

Married to whom _____ Year _____

Education:

High school _____ Year of graduation_____Scholastic degrees _____

College _____Year of graduation_____Scholastic degrees_____

Other Education_____Year of graduation_____Scholastic degrees _____

Occupations/Awards/Achievements:

Occupation _____ From _____ to _____

Previous occupation _____ From _____ to _____

Charitable organizations _____

Civic organizations _____

Awards/Achievements/Recognitions _____

Retired from _____

Personal Activities:

Church _____

Clubs/Fraternities _____

Hobbies _____

Favorite travel destinations: _____

Who will survive you? _____

Philosophy or private statement on life:_____

Figure 3-6 Personal Information Fact Sheet

If You're Stuck

If you get stuck and your parent digs in their heels and refuses to grant you Durable Power of Attorney, or if they refuse to deal with you on any of your attempts to help them through the legal maze, don't give up. Be patient, It may take some time for them to get used to the idea. They may not trust lawyers and they may not trust you or any other family member to handle their affairs. But to take your parent to court to battle it out for control of their finances is long, costly and usually a lose-lose situation. It can easily tear families apart. It's something that you probably don't want to get into.

If you've tried your best rational argument, tried peer pressure and family pressure, and your parent is still too stubborn to listen to your pleas for a setting up their legal affairs, you may feel disillusioned and frustrated. But don't give up on your parent just yet. Find it in your heart to forgive them, and accept them for who they are, not who you want them to be. Don't give up on your efforts. Eventually they'll probably come around.

CHAPTER 4

Housing – Finding the Best Option for Your Parent

As your parent grows older, their needs increase. If you're a part of helping them fulfill these needs, you may come to a point where you realize their needs for care have increased beyond your ability to effectively fill them. This may be especially true if you have a career or family, live more than a 30-minute drive from your parent, or cannot always be there for them on an as-needed basis. But how do you come to this realization, and how do you introduce a new idea like alternate housing options to your parent in a way they will likely accept? How can you explain to them all the housing options available in a way that will interest them but won't overwhelm them?

With my mom, she seemed happy living in her little tin box of a mobile home. She never complained, but I think she did become tired of cooking meals for herself. She never enjoyed cooking much anyway. On every visit, I began to notice she was eating more and more of her meals from a can. I also noticed that maintaining the small yard around her mobile home was beginning to stress her. Only a few years before, she enjoyed yard work. I also sensed that she might just be tired of living by herself – even though she claimed she loved her independence.

"With my mom, she seemed happy living in her little tin box of a mobile home."

For me, I felt depressed by the surroundings when I visited her. Her mobile home felt like a small, dark, lonely place illuminated only by the light of the television set – which seemed to be on 24 hours a day. Just imagining her cooped up in this place started to make me feel depressed. I managed to come by on weekends and help her with chores and provide conversation, but my weekends were also taken up with my own family's activities. To be truthful, I felt that I didn't have the time to spare for my mom that she seemed to need.

When she started to complain about her neighbors, it gave me an excuse to examine other housing options. My sister and I worked hard to find her a place where she had plenty of opportunities to make new friends and socialize with others like herself. We searched for a place that offered healthy home-cooked meals to replace her lonely dinner out of a can. Mom seemed receptive to the idea, so we started our search on the many housing options available for older people.

Starting your search for new housing for your parent seems to involve four choices:

1. Are they mentally receptive to the idea of moving?

2. Can you help them find a place they are likely to be happier at?

3. Can you identify the level of care available for their needs?

4. Can they, or their family, afford the place that offers the level of care they need?

In searching for a new home, my sister and I scoured the Yellow Pages and the Internet, looking for retirement homes, apartments, and other housing options. It took us about three weekends of touring available housing before we had a few choices to present to Mom. In that time we visited dozens of retirement homes, apartments, and private housing before we found the place we thought would be a good fit. Even though the place we found was a perfect fit at the time, within two years we had to move her again, this time to a facility where she could receive 24-hour care.

An incentive for moving may originate with you. It may also come as a suggestion from the doctor or gerontologist during a physical exam, as mentioned in Chapter 2. This recommendation may involve a combination of the following:

● Your parent is fine, and happy, where they are living now, but needs some minor assistance with chores or just the requirements of daily living. It may be recommended that some volunteers come to your parent's home. Or it may be suggested that your parent visit the senior center several times a week to get more social activity.

● It may be suggested that your parent might be more comfortable moving into a private apartment where meals are prepared, dishes are washed, and social activities are planned.

• If your parent needs major help, the doctor may recommend that they go directly to a hospital, nursing home, or private residential care facility. He may even recommend that a nurse be available on a 24-hour basis. Or he may suggest that a 24-hour non-medical care provider can fill your parent's need.

Obviously, the final choice on where your parent lives eventually belongs to your parent. As long as they are capable of making their own decisions, they will be the ones to decide where they want to live. If you let them be a major contributor in the decision process, they'll be a lot happier with the decision. I learned the hard way that you should never assume you know where it's best for your parent to live. It will eventually be their decision, even if they want to move into a dilapidated trailer park rather than into your new granny flat, as Mom did. You have to respect their reasons, even though they may not make a whole lot of sense to you at the time. You may be able to change their mind eventually and find better housing, but involving them in the choice will be crucial for the process to work. Try to think of yourself as the facilitator or negotiator, not the decision maker. You can always point out the downside of their decision if they are enamored with something that seems impractical - as they did with your ideas when you were growing up.

> "You may be able to change their mind eventually and find better housing, but involving them in the choice will be crucial for the process to work."

Option 1: Moving Your Parent in with You

Some families, usually in cultures other than the U.S., move their parent into their own home so they can look after them. If you have a good relationship with your parent, an extra room in your home, a loving heart, and time to look after them, you may want to consider this option. The time you'll have with your parent will either bring you closer or tear you apart. Caring for your parent can be one of the most rewarding, and sometimes one of the most brutally challenging things you can do in a lifetime.

Minor Improvements May Be All You Need

If you decide to take care of your parent in your own home, making the minor physical changes to upgrade your home to safety standards for an elderly or disabled person isn't that difficult. An extra grab bar in the bathroom, and a railing to help your parent up the front steps may be all that are needed. There are many good books with specifications of construction requirements for the handicapped is called These specifications are made up by the Americans with Disabilities Act (ADA) codes, and govern building requirements for Americans with disabilities throughout the U.S. With the knowledge of ADA requirements, you can make the necessary changes to add safety features to your current home so that it complies with ADA Standards and is a safer place for your aging parent to live.

Building a Granny Flat

If you don't have room inside your home for another person, consider adding a granny flat or a new bedroom and bathroom. A 20' x 20' granny flat with a bedroom, bathroom, heater, stove, cabinets, flooring, etc. can probably be built on your lot for around $20,000 – $35,000 depending on the location and style of construction. First, consult your local zoning authorities at City Hall because some areas don't allow granny flats, while other areas encourage them. Some communities even offer low-interest construction loans and financial assistance for building a granny flat. You can locate your local housing authority in the government pages in the phone book. Ask them if financial assistance is available for granny flats. Often, you can get back much of the money you put into an improvement such as a granny flat when you sell your home. And who knows, some day after your parent passes on, perhaps you can use it as a rental for extra money to fund your retirement, or as housing for a teenage son or daughter you may want a little distance from.

Finding a contractor who specializes in granny flats isn't difficult. The best contractors can be found by word of mouth, as most of them stay in business because of their reputation. Or you can find one in the Yellow Pages of your phone book. Be sure to get three bids on your granny flat project. Make sure you can approve and modify plans, within reason, before construction starts. Be sure you agree with the contractor on the price and that he sticks to the price listed on the bid as long as you don't make any changes once construction starts. Make sure there's a completion date listed in the contract.

It's also important to make sure the builder has built granny-flat type housing before. You don't want to have to educate him on how high the grab bars should be above the toilet and any other ADA building requirements. Get him to provide a list of references of past customers who are satisfied with his work. Be sure and call those references.

Make sure that you involve your parent in the project. You might want them to choose the carpets or drapes. Take their choices seriously, as the more they feel the place is theirs, the happier they're likely to be staying there.

Will Your Parent Be Happy With You, and You With Them?

Try considering whether your parent will be happier living with you than living alone or with someone else. Will you be there for them, or will you be at work all day, leaving them alone and isolated? Consider carefully if the two of you will be able to fit into each other's lifestyle. Does your parent require a lot of attention? Does your parent require a lot of personal space? Will they fit in with younger children in the home? Will your spouse be able to stand having your parent in your home, or near your home, after a year or two?

Each family is different. Moving a parent in with you usually requires more adjustment than just some remodeling or adding a room or granny flat to your cur-

> "Often, you can get back much of the money you put into an improvement such as a granny flat when you sell your home. And who knows, some day after your parent passes on, perhaps you can use it as a rental for extra money to fund your retirement, or as housing for a teenage son or daughter you may want a little distance from."

rent house. It often requires a change of lifestyle focused on caring for your parent. This change may be like a calling from God. If you feel it is your life's purpose to care for your parent and put aside your career, family, and your life to care for them, then you should sign up for the cause. Otherwise, you might want to consider helping them find a home elsewhere.

While moving your parent in with you may seem difficult, it can also be very rewarding. Not only can they be declared as dependents when you file your income taxes, but you'll have an important opportunity to know them better, and for them to know you better in the latter days of their life. It may be a rare opportunity in your life to do something good for another person – the same person that once made many sacrifices for you.

> "Moving a parent in with you usually requires more adjustment than just some remodeling or adding a room or granny flat to your current house. It often requires a change of lifestyle focused on caring for your parent."

If you have a demanding career or younger children who require a lot of attention, moving your parents in with you may not be the right thing to do. There's no need to feel guilty about this. It's better to come to grips with it early than to find out that you couldn't make it work after they've moved in. Then you'll really feel guilty. So consider it carefully and consult your family, because they will have to share any burden.

Not every family is emotionally suited to live in close proximity as they grow older. Not being emotionally close to your elderly parent isn't necessarily a bad thing. Sometimes you and your parent just feel more at ease with a little distance between you. This is the way it was with my mom, and it was why she chose not to move into our granny flat. Sometimes our effect on each other was discomfort if we were too close. If this is the story in your family, then it's unlikely that you or your parent are going to change at this late stage, even if you might like to. Chances are your parent will still want their independence, even if they need a walker or a wheelchair to get around. And chances are you will still feel uncomfortable with them living in close proximity — even if your intentions are good. There are other options to consider.

Option 2: Have Someone Come to Your Parent

If your parent needs minimal care, and you'd feel better having someone look after them when you can't be there, consider arranging for a nurse or other health care professional to check on them several times a week. This may cost from $600 to $800 per month depending on the number of visits and who comes to visit. Recent fees are $50 to $100 per hour for a registered nurse or nurse practitioner, $35 to $75 an hour for a licensed practical nurse or geriatric case manager, and $10 to $20 an hour for a home health aide. Night and weekend care may cost more. Having the care come to your parent's house may still cost less than moving them to a retirement home, depending on the amount of care required.

Does Medicare Pay for Home Health Visits?

In some cases Medicare will pay for at-home care. But there are restrictions. Here are some of them:

● Your parent's doctor has to arrange and set up the plan for your parent's home health care. Your parent's condition has to be serious enough to require skilled nursing care, not just help with cooking or bathing.

● Your parent has to show that it would require a considerable effort to leave their home to go to health care services and to certify that they are homebound.

Medicare will not pay for full-time nursing care, but usually pays for home care visits if the visits are intermittent skilled nursing care or therapy. Make sure Medicare has certified the home health agency that provides home-care services for your parent.

To find a home-visit nurse, ask your doctor, call your local hospital, or consult a professional geriatric care manager who is trained to locate, coordinate, and supervise care. A geriatric care manager can usually save you the cost of their fee by providing you with help in applying for Medicare benefits and finding less-expensive resources and help for your parent. These pros can help you find the loopholes and steer you to the best care for your parent at the least price. You can find geriatric care managers in the phone book, through the senior center resources, or through your local Eldercare directory.

There are home health care agencies that can provide personnel to help your parent at home with general chores such as bathing, eating, dressing, and toileting. Sometimes these agencies will charge your parent, and sometimes they are partially funded by the state you reside in. Some are funded by religious organizations. Look in the Yellow Pages of your phone book to find them.

If your parent needs full-time care and doesn't want to go to a nursing home, there are special live-in nurses that provide one-on-one care. A live-in nurse might cost as much or more than it would cost to have your parent stay in a nursing home, but it's an option that will let your parent stay in their own home. A good live-in nurse can provide top-notch care if you or your parent can afford it.

Roommates

There is also the possibility of finding a roommate for your parent, especially if they have an extra bedroom or two. There may be a person your parent's age, or a little younger, out there in the community who is looking for shared housing. Put an ad on the bulletin board at your local senior center, local or community college, or even in the local newspaper. You might be surprised at the number of applicants. Ask each applicant to fill out an application. You can use the sample application shown in Figure 4-1. Make sure the applicant signs the bottom line, giving you permission to check their references. Call the previous landlord as well as the one where they are living now. The landlord at a previous residence is much more likely to give you a true reference on a potential roommate, than the current landlord, who might see an opportunity to rid himself of a bad tenant.

This form included on the disk in the back of this book.

Don't be enamored by a prospective roommate, as first-time impressions with potential roommates can be deceiving. Try for you and your parent to use both your rational and emotional mind. Remember, you're looking for a compassionate person, someone your parent can get along with, as well as someone who has a proven record of responsible behavior.

Rental Application Form

Name_____ Home phone_____ Work phone _____

Social security #_____ Date of birth_____

Current address_____City/State/Zip_____

How long? _____ Why leaving? _____

Owner/Manager/Landlord_____ Phone _____

Previous address_____City/State/Zip_____

How long at this address? _____ Rent paid? _____

Reason for leaving? _____

Owner/Manager/Landlord_____ Phone _____

Any pets? _____ Please describe_____

Employer_____ Phone_____ How long? _____

Occupation_____ Net income_____ per [ ] month [ ] year

Bank name_____Branch_____ Account #_____

Major credit card_____ Balance _____ Monthly payment_____

Major credit card_____ Balance _____ Monthly payment_____

Major credit card_____ Balance _____ Monthly payment_____

Have you ever applied for bankruptcy? _____ Have you ever been evicted or asked to leave a rental? _____

Have you ever been arrested? _____ Have you ever paid a late fee? _____ Do you smoke? _____

Number of vehicles_____ Make _____Year_____ License number _____

Make _____Year _____ License number _____

Name and relationship of every person who lives with you (include ages of minor children)_____

IN EVENT OF EMERGENCY NOTIFY:

Name_____ Relationship_____ Address_____ Phone_____

In signing this application I give approval to check my credit and all information written here to determine eligibility for this rental unit.

Applicant _____ Date_____

Figure 4-1 Rental Application Form

If you've found someone you feel is exceptional, call a credit agency such as Triple A Credit, at 1-800-576-1111, and get a credit check. This will cost you around $20, but it will give you factual information about the person, such as whether they are financially mature enough to pay their bills on time. Paying an agency such Triple A Credit to look up credit information will give you their interpretation of whether the potential roommate is financially mature. They've seen enough credit reports to make a judgment call. You can also apply for credit information on the Internet, but you'll have to decipher what all the data means. I've found that can be difficult. I think it's worth a few extra dollars to have a professional agency give their interpretation of a credit report on a person.

However, you probably aren't going to get your parent a roommate with a perfect credit report. But the credit report will tell you if they pay their bills. I've found that as a rule of thumb, a person who is responsible enough to pay their bills on time tends to be responsible in other areas of their life. There are always exceptions to the rule, but since you're putting your parent into the hands of a complete stranger, you might as well pay $20, to at least find if that stranger pays their bills.

Once you and your parent have found the right person, write up a month-to-month rental agreement to spell out all the responsibilities that come with being a roommate, such as taking out the trash, washing dirty dishes, doing laundry, etc. There's a sample rental agreement shown in Figure 4-2. Enter all of your parent's expectations in writing so there's no chance for misunderstandings later. Then, you (if you're managing or brokering this agreement), your parent, and the potential roommate should sign the rental agreement.

This form included on the disk in the back of this book.

Roommates tend to be temporary. It can be difficult to find a match that lasts more than six months. Petty grievances can fester and grow into major problems, especially if the roommate isn't emotionally mature. If your parent isn't used to having other people around, they may experience difficulty adjusting to another person's habits – no matter how well they seemed to match initially.

Live-in Care

If your parent is happy at home, has an extra bedroom, and needs a little care, there is also the possibility of getting someone to provide live-in care in exchange for room and board. This can be anyone from a college student looking for room and board, to an older person looking for companionship. In this arrangement, your parent rents out an extra room in exchange for someone to do chores such as shopping, washing dishes, cleaning, yard work, and transportation.

Roommate Agreement Form

This Agreement entered into on (date)_____ between _____ (roommate) and _____ (landlord). Landlord rents to roommate one bedroom and shared kitchen and bathroom facilities on the premises located at _____ together with the following furnishings and appliances_____.

The premises are to be used only as a private residence for roommate listed above and landlord listed above. Occupancy by guests for more than one day at a time without the landlord's written permission is prohibited and will be considered a breach of this contract.

The rental will begin on _____ and continue on a month-to-month basis. Landlord may put an end to the tenancy or modify the terms of this agreement by giving the roommate 30 days written notice. Roommate may likewise end this agreement by giving the landlord 30 days written notice.

Roommate agrees to pay $ _____, payable in advance on the first day of each month. Rent will be paid in person to: _____. Landlord will accept personal checks, cash, or money order as methods of payment for rent. If roommate fails to pay the rent in full by the fourth day after it is due, landlord may charge a late fee of $_____. The total late charge for any one month may not exceed $____.

On signing this agreement, roommate agrees to pay landlord $_____ as a security deposit. Roommate may not, without landlord's written consent, use this security deposit, as rent.

Roommate agrees to the following responsibilities in return for renting a room at said premises.

1) Agrees to clean all dishes after use and not to leave them unwashed in the sink.

2) Agrees to clean their room in a reasonable manner.

3) Agrees to leave bathroom in the manner in which they found it. For example, toothpaste not left in sink, hairbrushes not left on floor, etc.

4) Agrees to help Landlord by offering the following services_____

5)_____

Roommate is entitled to quiet enjoyment of the premises except for: _____. Roommate agrees to not create a nuisance with loud noises, annoyances, or disturbances that would disturb the landlord.

Landlord may enter roommate's premises in the event of emergency, or to make repairs or improvements. Except for emergencies, landlord will give tenant 24 hours notice before entering roommate's premises.

Roommate acknowledges, agrees to, has receipt of, and has read a copy of this agreement.

Landlord Signature_____ Date_____

Broker Signature_____ Date_____

Phone: _____

Roommate Signature: _____ Date_____

Current Address_____ City/State/Zip_____

Phone: _____

Figure 4-2 Roommate Agreement Form

Web Sites of National Organizations for Housing

www.nationalsharedhousing.org is the Web site of National Shared Housing, a nonprofit foundation that helps seniors find shared housing. They have chapters in practically every city of every state. Call the number listed on the Web site for the chapter closest to you.

www.aahsa.org will take you to the American Association of Homes and Services for the Aging. This is a non-profit organization representing 5,600 not-for-profit nursing homes, retirement communities, and senior housing facilities across the U.S. They provide an excellent publication called the Consumer's Directory of Continuing Care Retirement Communities, which lists retirement communities across the U.S. There's also a great consumer information page on their Web site with links to medical articles, consumer information about health care, options for a relative with Alzheimer's disease, and consumer tips on finding an assisted living home.

www.ccal.org will take you to the Consumer Consortium on Assisted Living, a national, non-profit organization representing the needs of consumers in assisted living facilities, and educating professionals and the general public on assisted living issues. They have a checklist called "Questions to Ask When Choosing an Assisted Living Facility" that you can download from their Web site.information.

(continued on next page)

This arrangement seems to work well with responsible college students looking for low-cost housing in exchange for assuming some limited responsibilities. I remember it appeared attractive when I was a poor, starving college student. Unlike the roommate situation mentioned earlier, a "live-in" pays a low rent but in exchange, agrees to perform certain duties to help your parent with daily tasks. Your parent may pay for food, and utilities, or you may itemize them as separate expenses, depending on the agreement you wish to set up. The important thing is that your parent has another person in the house to help them in some of their daily tasks.

Make sure all the duties are outlined in the rental agreement, and that everyone has a clear understanding of their role in advance. Also, be sure to carefully check references. You want to make sure the person is trustworthy and dependable. To locate potential live-in care roommates call a nearby community or state college or university and talk to the housing office.

One downside of a roommate or live-in care arrangement is that it can be a temporary solution to a long-term problem. Most roommates or live-in renters don't last long. They may move out on you just when your parent needs them most. But there is a possibility that by offering someone the chance, you may find just the right person and your parent and this person may establish a beautiful relationship. After all, that's what life is all about, those beautiful relationships, even if your parent may have to take a chance and open up to a stranger.

Option 3: Foster Care

Sometimes you can find a family willing to take in an older person, much as a foster-care family takes in children. This arrangement usually costs from $500 to $4,000 a month, but the family should provide your parent with meals, a private room, laundry, and transportation as well as a loving relationship.

Option 4: A Senior Apartment

If your parent is independent and comfortable living on their own but just wants to be closer or nearer to other people, consider a senior apartment. Senior apartments have many advantages. Your parent will be living with many others of the same age, so they're bound to make a friend or two. Senior apartments are usually close to shopping, movies, and transportation. Some even provide social activities. Many provide laundry services and meals. They should also provide some kind of security and crime prevention.

Moving your parent to a senior apartment may require some adjustments, especially if your parent has been living a rural life. It may take some time for them to get used to hearing another person walking on their ceiling. But the minor inconveniences will be overshadowed by the advantages offered by a senior apartment. Senior apartments are like poor-man's retirement homes. In fact, sometimes they are only available to low-income people. Many are government subsidized and have waiting lists that stretch on for years. If your parent doesn't have much retirement income, but wants to have more fun and be with others their own age, you may want to check up on a senior apartment.

You can find senior apartments listed in the Yellow Pages of your phone book or in a directory usually published by your local senior center. Check the location first to make sure the neighborhood is safe. These apartments are usually located in urban neighborhoods that may not be first-class, though you can find some in acceptable locations. Conduct a lone surveillance tour. Walk into the lobby. Usually there will be a volunteer guard at the door to find out what you're doing there. Be candid and tell him you're checking the place out for your parent. Take the tour or take the elevator up yourself. When you walk through the apartment make a note, does it appear to be a warm, fresh-smelling place? Be sure and ask yourself if your parent would be happy there.

Some senior apartments can be cold, dark, and dreary, with a musty old smell that permeates the walls. They can also act as a magnet for criminals who prey on older people.

Web Sites of National Organizations for Housing (continued)

www.seniorhousing.net also has a complete listing of retirement homes in your area with prices and photos of their exteriors. In some cases, you can look at actual 360 degree virtual tours of available senior housing including rooms, lobby, and other areas. This Web site is chock full of useful information. It has a great interactive checklist for evaluating the best type of housing or care for your parent. It explains the differences in housing options that are available and offers checklists for evaluating a senior housing or care center. It also lists storage facilities throughout the U.S. and Canada. It has one of the best links to medical sites I've seen.

www.livon.com has interactive health checklists that show you the level of care your parent will require. Then you can go through a list of housing and search by location, level of care, and price. You can find photos and floor plans of the facilities. You can even send an instant request for a facility's brochure or an on-site tour. This Web site lists available senior services.

"Usually there will be a volunteer guard at the door to find out what you are doing there."

Sample Evaluation Checklist for a Senior Apartment

Apartment name_____ Address_____

Price per month: _____ Phone_____

Rating	Great	Reasonable	Not so great
Location of facility	☐	☐	☐
Lighting & cleanliness	☐	☐	☐
Security	☐	☐	☐
Smell of elevator	☐	☐	☐
Residents in facility	☐	☐	☐
Available transportation	☐	☐	☐
Government assistance	☐	☐	☐
Length of waiting list	☐	☐	☐
Amenities included	☐	☐	☐
Overall impression	☐	☐	☐

Other_____

Other_____

Other_____

Notes and impressions: _____

_____

Figure 4-3 Sample Evaluation Checklist for a Senior Apartment

This form included on the disk in the back of this book.

On your surveillance tour, take a walk through the neighborhood. Are the houses well maintained? Are there bars over the windows of the homes? Do the neighbors appear friendly and helpful? You can use Figure 4-3 to help you evaluate a senior apartment.

How Much Does a Senior Apartment Cost?

A senior apartment can be government subsidized and cost as little as $150 to as much as $2,500 per month, depending on the location and type of housing.

Option 5: An Independent-Living Retirement Home

These are usually apartment-type complexes, which are well maintained and quiet. For a fixed monthly fee a resident is treated to two or three meals a day in a restaurant-style setting. Most feature exercise programs such as yoga and tai chi, golf, and weekly outings to plays or movies. Transportation is usually provided by a van owned by the complex. Some provide morning walks. Some even have their own golf courses. Most have beauty salons on site. Some facilities even have live bands playing Swing, Dixieland, and jazz concerts several nights a month. Some have their own happy hours, libraries, and chapels. Every holiday becomes a main event that shifts the social director into overdrive with new exciting programs that encourage socialization and fun. Some of these retirement homes are like cruise ships on land. If your parent socializes well with others, they'll fit right in, as the opportunities for socialization abound here. If your parent is a loner, you may be paying for services they won't use. It's unlikely they'll change to a social butterfly at this late stage of their life.

"Some of these retirement homes are like cruise ships on land."

What the Rooms Are Like

Most of the rooms seem like tiny apartments, with small kitchens and a private bath. Moving from a private home to one of these tiny apartments can be a big adjustment, and you may have to rent storage space for many of your parent's possessions if they want to hold on to them. But the many social opportunities offered in this type of retirement oasis can sometimes overcome the sacrifice. If your parent lacks friends, these places offer plenty of opportunities for them to meet and share activities with others like them. You can always rent out or sell your parent's old home to help make the rental payments at one of these retirement communities.

How Much Does an Independent Living Retirement Home Cost?

Costs vary on location, type of programs available, and the amount of experience of the staff. Figure on somewhere from $1,000 to $3,500 per month. But keep in mind that this cost covers just about everything – even transportation to medical appointments. Medical and dental care, hair care, beauty treatments, and food kept in the apartment usually aren't covered.

Evaluation Checklist for an Independent-Living Retirement Home

Name of facility_____ Address_____

Price per month: _____ Phone_____

Rating	Great	Reasonable	Not so great
Location of facility	☐	☐	☐
Lighting & cleanliness	☐	☐	☐
Security	☐	☐	☐
Smell of lobby	☐	☐	☐
Residents in facility	☐	☐	☐
Transportation provided	☐	☐	☐
Social calendar	☐	☐	☐
Facility staff	☐	☐	☐
Meals	☐	☐	☐
Available rooms	☐	☐	☐
Hair salon	☐	☐	☐
Overall impression	☐	☐	☐

Is assisted living provided?　yes ☐　no ☐

Special dietary needs OK?　yes ☐　no ☐

	Great	Reasonable	Not so great
Overall impression	☐	☐	☐

Other_____

Other_____

Other_____

Notes and impressions: _____

_____

_____

_____

Figure 4-4 Evaluation Checklist for an Independent-Living Retirement Home

How to Find a Good Independent Living Retirement Home

Look in the Yellow Pages of your phone book and write down the addresses of five retirement homes. Don't pick the ones with the largest ads — they're likely to be the most expensive, but not necessarily the best. Also check the Web site www.seniorhousing.net or the Web sites listed previously. Take a Saturday morning and go visit a few of these homes, completely unannounced. Linger in the lobby and use your nose as a guide. Does it smell fresh? Or does it smell stale and musty? Is there fresh coffee and newspapers for residents?

Look at the residents. Ask yourself "Are they happy to be living here?" Do they smile at you when you smile at them, or do they stare straight ahead? Watch how the residents interact with the staff. Do they interact in a friendly way or is it suspicious and guarded? The staff of a retirement home can make or break the social environment. If they seem to relate well and professionally with the residents, chances are you've found a good place.

Then go to the front desk and tell them you'd like a tour. Usually, they'll take you to a marketing person who will appear interested and friendly (that's their job). They'll walk you around and introduce you to the other staff members. Look these people in the eye. Are they friendly, or are they just trying to sell you something? Do you feel they are trustworthy? Are they professional? Would you feel comfortable leaving your parent in their hands? You can use Figure 4-4 to help you evaluate an independent-living retirement home.

The choice of a retirement home is really based on your objective and subjective evaluation. Once you've picked a few favorites, get one of your family members to come along with you and your parent to do the final inspection. It's more effective to scout ahead on a lone reconnaissance tour before dragging along the troops.

Check prices because they can vary widely. Also, you might consider checking out a neighboring town if you can find a better home for less. As in the game of Monopoly, Boardwalk and Park Place may be great areas for a retirement home, but if your parent can't afford it, check out a few on what may be

Retirement Apartments

In my hunt for an independent living retirement apartment I found these five totally different types:

1. A new home managed by aging hippies who had long hair and flowing skirts. The maintenance personnel all sported a variety of tattoos. Incense was burning in one of the rooms. It was an inexpensive place to live. In fact, it was a downright bargain. But I didn't want to leave my mom there.

2. An aging high-rise apartment building that reeked of mold and urine. Although it had a good reputation among the elderly in the community, no one was available to give me a tour without an appointment. They were too busy. To me, the residents appeared lonely, like they were in a place that time had forgotten. I could easily imagine most of them were stuck in their rooms watching black & white TV.

3. A family-managed place that seemed well maintained. However the staff permitted older 'disabled' children to stay with the residents if the children could be classified as 'disabled'. Several of these 'disabled' children were in their late 30's and were having a beer bust when I visited.

4. A religious-based retirement home. This home seemed to have high moral standards. The caretakers seemed to care for the guests. The price was reasonable. It had a great garden area. But it was old and smelled musty. I marked it down to take my mom there and let her decide for herself.

5. A well-run home staffed by professionals, where guests and staff seemed happy and the smell was clean and fresh. Posters of photos from their last successful social function were on display. The pool was well-maintained with a large group of male residents actually in it. It cost slightly more than the others but seemed well worth it. And it was.

> "It's important is to find a place for your parent within a 30-minute drive of your own home. As time progresses, you'll probably be spending more time visiting there."

Atlantic, or even Vermont Avenue. Sometimes a little time spent shopping can turn up a real bargain in another town, which, while still close to you, can offer more for less money.

Most independent-living retirement homes are like an oasis in the desert, and they're built like a fortress with a courtyard in the middle. Chances are your parent will put more emphasis on the services and the people on the inside than on the actual physical location – especially if the complex offers transportation, so they don't have to drive their own car any more.

It's important to find a place for your parent within a 30-minute drive of your own home. As time progresses, you'll probably be spending more time visiting there, so you want it to be close by.

Looking back at my own mom, I'm glad that she had the opportunity to stay in one of these communities before moving on to a board and care home. At least we were able to help her out of a lonely existence and into a whirlwind of socialization, if only for a few years. Knowing what I know now, I wish we had applied pressure on her to move sooner than we did.

Downside of an Independent Living Retirement Home

If your parent has been living alone, you'll usually have to rent storage space for their belongings. Many of these belongings may end up at your place. Later, after your parent is settled, they may decide they don't need some of their belongings any more, and you can sell them to help pay for their needs.

If your parent was used to a rural life, they'll have to adjust to the noises of apartment living, such as the sound of toilets flushing. The natural sounds of birds may be replaced by the perpetual sound of their neighbor's TV.

Also, if they've been living alone for a while, it may be difficult for them to get used to dinner arriving on schedule every night – whether they're hungry or not.

Try to look at each facility you check out as a place your parent may not want to move from again. Moving to a new home is difficult for anyone. And it doesn't get any easier as you get older.

This form included on the disk in the back of this book.

Can Your Parent Afford an Independent Living Retirement Home?

The biggest problem with this type of housing is usually its cost. Can they actually afford it? Can you help them afford it? Will it be worth the hassle of the move? Will they really fit in with the crowd there? Will it be worth the extra money for them to live there? To find out, add up all their current expenses (including car insurance, utilities, and food) and see how much more it will actually cost them. Use the worksheet in Figure 4-5.

Monthly Income and Expense Worksheet

List all sources of income that your parent is receiving, including Social Security, royalty, rents, and pension.

Income Source	Monthly Amount
Pension	_____
Social Security	_____
Rental income	_____
Annuity	_____
Bonds	_____
Other	_____
Other	_____
Total monthly income	_____

List all of your parent's monthly expenses

Expense	Monthly Amount
Rent/house payment	_____
House maintenance	_____
Utilities	_____
Yard maintenance	_____
Phone	_____
Food	_____
Restaurants	_____
Transportation	_____
Car insurance/maintenance	_____
Doctor	_____
Prescriptions	_____
Beauty salon	_____
Pet supplies and expenses	_____
Other	_____
Total monthly expense	_____

Figure 4-5 Monthly Income and Expense Worksheet

This record is for your use, as you may have to help your parent liquidate some of these assets to provide them with a better way of life. It's also good for you to know what assets your parent has, just in case you have to take charge of them some day. Also, completing this form will help you become aware of some of the debts your parent may have incurred.

This form included on the disk in the back of this book.

Remember, most older people have assets set aside somewhere. Your job here is to help them improve their lifestyle, using the assets they have. Use the Personal Financial Worksheet shown in Figure 4-6 to help locate hidden assets you may be able to use at this time. Sometimes it's a formidable task, but usually, if you try hard, you'll find a way.

Assisted Living in an Independent Living Retirement Home

Some independent retirement homes have a wing or special section called the assisted living section. While the name sounds scary and expensive, it's not that bad. Having an assisted living section in a retirement home adds one more level of care should your parent need it. It also means that there is usually a full-time nurse on the grounds should your parent need a quick medical assessment. Your parent could be staying in the independent living section and just need a little extra help. An aide from the assisted living section can dispense medications or help with bathing or showering. This usually involves an extra monthly fee, but it's still considerably cheaper than moving your parent to a full-blown nursing home, where you're paying for all of the expensive amenities your parent doesn't need.

As time progresses, your parent may begin to need more help from the assisted living personnel. If this happens it may be your wake up call announcing that it's time to start checking around for alternative housing. This is especially true if you notice that your parent isn't taking part in the social activities provided by their retirement community. There are alternative living situations, which may cost less, and at the same time offer more care for your parent.

"As time progresses, your parent may begin to need more help from the assisted living personnel. If this happens it may be your wake up call announcing that it's time to start checking around for alternative housing."

My mom's decline became noticeable when she started having trouble meeting the dinner schedule at her independent living retirement home. Then one night she fell and ended up in the hospital. We suspect this was from taking a double dose of her medications, and started paying an orderly to dispense her medications every morning, just to be safe. I noticed that over time she became more and more withdrawn, and her memory was getting worse. Even our efforts at bribing the social director to drag her out of her room and into activities were failing.

When we took her for a geriatric evaluation, it was recommended that she receive 24-hour care. These changes in her mental deterioration came in stages over time. Looking back now, they were very apparent. But at the time, they crept up so gradually we hardly realized what was happening until they became acute.

Personal Financial Worksheet

Asset   **Possible Value (low estimate)**

Home   _____

Car(s)   _____

Appliances   _____

Jewelry   _____

Other   _____

Other   _____

Bank Accounts (include checking, savings, money market, & CDs)

Name of Bank _____Account #_____ Current Account Value_____

Name of Bank _____Account #_____ Current Account Value_____

Name of Bank _____Account #_____ Current Account Value_____

Name of Bank _____Account #_____ Current Account Value_____

Other Investments (include bonds, saving bonds, Treasury notes, stocks, mutual funds, and other investments)

Type	Purchase Date	Maturity Date	Value	Yield
_____	_____	_____	_____	_____
_____	_____	_____	_____	_____
_____	_____	_____	_____	_____

Tax-Deferred Accounts (include limited partnerships, annuities, IRAs, Keogh profit-sharing plans, pension plans)

Type	Date Received	Value	Monthly Income
_____	_____	_____	_____
_____	_____	_____	_____

Real Property (include land, homes, and mobile homes)

Type	Appraised Value
_____	_____
_____	_____
_____	_____

Figure 4-6 Personal Financial Worksheet

Personal Financial Worksheet (continued)

Real Property (include land, homes, and mobile homes)

Type   Appraised Value

_____   _____

_____   _____

_____   _____

_____   _____

_____   _____

Parent's Debts (include mortgages, auto loans, credit cards, and all other personal debts)

Type	Lender	Date Due	Amount Owed
_____	_____	_____	_____
_____	_____	_____	_____
_____	_____	_____	_____
_____	_____	_____	_____

Figure 4-6 Personal Financial Worksheet (continued)

Option 6: A Three-Part Care Facility

Some larger retirement homes are set up with three levels of care. There may be an independent living section located in a wing of the facility. The residents in this wing come and go as they choose. They take field trips and social outings to movies and plays. Then, as they need more care, they move into another section – assisted living, which is located in another wing of the same retirement home. The assisted living wing may be like a mini-nursing home. It's usually staffed with full-time nurses. My mom was actually at this level of care at her independent living home when we started to pay someone to dispense medication.

Finally, there is a wing of the facility that's locked. This wing provides the third level of care, 24 hours a day, for demented and Alzheimer's patients. Occasionally, a three-part care facility will have a full-scale nursing home, and even a hospice and a funeral home.

These facilities can be huge. Besides the amount of activities they offer, they usually have so many people in them that your parent is bound to meet someone like themself. Having a full-time nursing staff on duty is an added plus, especially when something goes wrong in the middle of the night.

Downside of a Three-Part Care Facility

The downside of a three-part care facility is that it can be so large that things get lost in the shuffle. Nurses may be rotated before they can get to know their patients. Your parent may not get the best care in that type of situation. I've known people who have taken their parent out of a large institutional setting and are much happier with the care their parent receives at a smaller residential care facility. There's also another factor – when you place all people under one roof – residents requiring the maximum level of care with those requiring little or no extra care – it doesn't create a great mix. But it really depends on how your parent feels about it, since they're the one who'll be living there.

How Much Does a Three-Part Facility Cost?

Three-part care facilities usually start out at the same level as retirement homes – around $1,600 to $4,500 per month. The price goes up with the level of care needed. The overhead on such a huge place is usually high, with lots of doctors and nurses on staff, and those overhead costs are passed on to the residents.

> "The downside of a three-part care facility is that it can be so large that things get lost in the shuffle. Nurses may be rotated before they can get to know their patients."

Feel free to check out a few of these medical metropolises for your own education. Go unannounced on a Saturday for a solo fact-finding visit. They're usually happy to take you on a tour. Check with your nose as well as your eyes. Do you smell excrement or urine? Or do you smell bleach and disinfectant? Does the staff have the ability to easily communicate with your parent? Do they speak the same language with enough ability to eliminate misunderstandings? Are the residents happy? Would you feel comfortable leaving your parent there? If you're happy with what you see, make an appointment to bring your parent back along with your family for an official tour.

Option 7: A Board and Care Home

Not many people are familiar with board and care homes. These places can provide 24-hour care for your parent with a variety of outings and social activities. They are usually located in private homes where up to six older people live in a family-type setting. Meals are provided, as is transportation to the doctor's office, hairdresser, and sometimes movies and plays. Some even provide ocean or lake cruises. Trained employees, called caregivers, provide care to residents. They aren't skilled nurses, but they are special people who devote their lives to caring for people like your parent. Usually each caregiver has a shift of time when they're on duty. They usually sleep downstairs or somewhere close by in case they're needed during the night.

In a good board and care home, a family-type atmosphere prevails. The residents will care for each other as family. These homes are like a normal boarding house but with set rules, a leader, and an agenda. Board and care facilities are usually licensed by the state and have to follow fairly strict rules and guidelines to stay in business. A board and care home will keep voluminous files on its residents so that if anything goes wrong – they'll have it covered. Also, the state usually has strict licensing requirements for these homes and will follow up with surprise periodic inspections.

Board and care homes group the people living in each home by the amount of care they require. Your parent would usually stay in a home with other residents needing the same level of care. This works to everyone's advantage, as your parent will make friends with other residents, and hopefully become a member of the family. As your parent ages and requires more care, they can move to another board and care facility where they're with others who require that same level of care.

Board and care homes are operated by private citizens who are individual entrepreneurs. Since these are small-time operations, the level of care they provide ranges dramatically. Unlike the large institutional care facilities, there is no board of directors, no marketing or social director. It's one chief who wears a lot of hats, and has a whole lot of employees working under him or her.

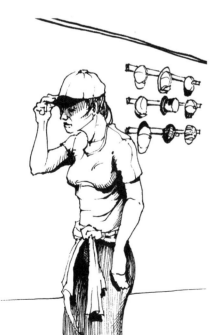

"It's one chief who wears a lot of hats, and has a whole lot of employees working under him or her."

A good board and care place can provide a level of care not found at a larger facility. The caregivers usually have fewer people to look after, so they get to know each person as an individual, and can care for them in a more personalized way. If there are changes in your parent's behavior or health, the caregiver may notice it before you do, and call you to request permission to take your parent to the doctor.

Another thing about a good residential board and care facility is that usually it has operated in the community for years. Over those years it has developed a support network of geriatric doctors, nurses, and medical suppliers. Through this support network the board and care home can recommend a wide range of top-notch geriatric health care providers. These recommendations may include doctors, nurses, lawyers, notary publics, dentists, and hairdressers. This can be a real Godsend if you're busy with a family or career and your parent suddenly needs a dentist, doctor, or nurse. Many times the residential board and care staff will take your parent to the doctor or the dentist, or even the hospital, and be there with them through the whole procedure when you can't. This is just a part of the service that a good board and care residential facility can provide.

In a residential board and care facility, your parent will usually get more intensive care that can actually cost considerably less than what they'd pay in a larger facility. If you want to avoid an expensive nursing home for a while, consider a residential board and care home. They cost much less than a nursing home. While they don't provide 24-hour nursing care, they may offer better over-all care.

One of the most efficient things about a board and care residential facility is that the director is usually available to answer questions. When so many things can happen to your parent, you're probably going to have a lot of questions.

How Much Does a Board and Care Facility Cost?

Residential board and care facilities usually start out at the same level as retirement homes – around $1,200 to 2,500 per month. The price goes up with the level of care required.

How to Find a Good Board and Care Facility

Residential board and care homes can be hard to find. They don't run full-page ads in your Sunday newspaper, and often don't have Web pages. They usually have very small advertising budgets and rely on reputation and word of mouth advertising. There may be publications available through social services or the senior center in your community that list phone numbers of board and care facilities. Many times you can find out about board and care homes through social workers or geriatric counselors. Sometimes hospitals or geriatric clinics will refer them to you.

The first action to take to find a good residential board and care is to call a residential care director and set up an appointment for a meeting. A residential care director will usually be responsible for more than one board and care facility. He'll ask you about specific medical needs that your parent has and the type of care they'll need. Then he'll try to make a match with your parent and a home that has a room available.

Most residential board and care homes are just homes in the community. They probably won't have a sign in the front yard, and they'll look like every other house in the neighborhood, except for something like a handrail up to the front porch.

> "In a residential board and care facility, your parent will usually get more intensive care that can actually cost considerably less than what they'd pay in a larger facility."

As you walk in the front door, ask yourself if it feels like a happy place? Would you feel comfortable coming there at any time of day to visit your parent? Do the residents seem happy? Does the staff accept them all? Are they getting enough exercise or are they stuck like zombies in front of the TV all day?

My personal grudge against board and care facilities is that the television can become an adult baby sitter. Some of the places I visited had giant-screen TVs tuned to soap operas all day long. Every resident had a favorite chair where they remained planted throughout the day.

While having everyone stuck in front of a TV may make it easy for the caregivers, it isn't too healthy for the residents. My mom stayed at one of these for a while. My sister and I had to come on weekends to try and take Mom for a walk, to get her away from the television, and give her a little physical exercise.

"My personal grudge against board and care facilities is that the television can become an adult baby sitter."

Take a look at the social calendar for the facility. It should be posted in clear sight on a wall. Are there activities your parent would enjoy? Do they take the residents out to lunch occasionally, to the movies, to the hairdresser, to outings of some kind?

Also check the meals provided. Are they receiving lots of green vegetables and roughage? As the body ages and gets less exercise, regularity can become a problem. Does the diet contain lots of starchy foods with little roughage? Or does it provide good nutrition that features salads and bran? You don't want your parent to wind up with a blocked colon. A blocked colon is a fairly common problem among older people and can be a life-threatening situation. Ask the caregivers if they're willing to serve salads and bran daily. If they give you a blank stare, move on.

Find out if cranberry juice is regularly on the menu. Why? Older people, especially older women, are very susceptible to urinary tract infections. These infections can go undiagnosed for months and can affect the balance of electrolytes in the body. This can lead to some very strange symptoms that may be difficult to diagnose, and can make you believe your parent is at death's door. Yet, all they have is a urinary tract infection – easily treated with an antibiotic or sulfa drug. Cranberry juice has been shown to help prevent or reduce the severity of urinary tract infections. Hopefully, the care facility already knows this. A board and care facility should be flexible enough to add bran or cranberry juice to your parent's diet if you ask for it. Ask questions and find out.

Evaluation Checklist for a Residential Board & Care Facility

Name of facility_____ Address_____

Price per month_____ Phone: _____

	Great	Reasonable	Not so great	Notes
Location of facility	☐	☐	☐	_____
Lighting & cleanliness	☐	☐	☐	_____
Caregivers	☐	☐	☐	_____
Smell	☐	☐	☐	_____
Dining room	☐	☐	☐	_____
Residents in facility	☐	☐	☐	_____
Transportation	☐	☐	☐	_____
Entertainment/activities	☐	☐	☐	_____
Social calendar	☐	☐	☐	_____
Facility staff	☐	☐	☐	_____
Meals/diet	☐	☐	☐	_____
Available rooms	☐	☐	☐	_____
Hair salon	☐	☐	☐	_____
Exercise	☐	☐	☐	_____

Pertinent Questions to Ask

	Yes	No
Special assistance provided?	☐	☐
Special dietary needs ok?	☐	☐
Do caregivers speak clearly in your parent's language?	☐	☐
Can you examine the licensing reports for the home?	☐	☐
Are the costs for any care beyond basic care clear?	☐	☐
Does the facility offer hospice care?	☐	☐
Can your parent keep their own physician?	☐	☐
Do you have to call ahead to visit your parent?	☐	☐
Can your parent use their own furniture & TV?	☐	☐
Can your parent have their own phone?	☐	☐
Can your parent have a pet?	☐	☐
Does the home provide overnight staffing?	☐	☐
Can family members occasionally join in on meals?	☐	☐

Notes and impressions: _____

Figure 4-7 Evaluation Checklist for a Residential Board & Care Facility

This form included on the disk in the back of this book.

Get several references from families whose parents have stayed in the facility. While you're touring – especially if it's on a weekend – you may even meet a few families at the facility. Take them aside and ask them how long their parent has been there. Ask them how they feel about leaving their parent there. Check out at least three board and care facilities before settling on one. You can use Figure 4-7 to help you evaluate them.

Once you settle on a residential board and care home you like, give the director a copy of your list of medications from Chapter 1. They'll keep a folder of your parent's medical history, along with special dietary needs or requests (such as lots of salads and cranberry juice). Because a board and care facility is small, they should be able to customize the care for each resident.

"When you do get to the point where you take responsibility for the location of your parent's new home, doubts always seem to creep in about your decision – no matter how much you may have researched the new venue."

Living With Your Housing Decision

Finding a place for your parent to stay can be an on-going challenge as they grow older. But whether it's your own granny flat, live-in care, senior apartment, retirement home, independent living, or residential board and care, finding the right residence that you and your parent are comfortable with is one of the most important decisions you can make. At first, this decision will probably heavily involve your parent. Later, if their ability to make decisions diminishes, it will be primarily your own effort with the help of your family. Hopefully, some of the information here will be useful and help you prevent some of the mistakes that my sister and I made.

When you do get to the point where you take responsibility for the location of your parent's new home, doubts always seem to creep in about your decision – no matter how much you may have researched the new venue. Making permanent choices that affect the lives of others are never easy.

For my sister and I, when we were against a deadline, trying to find our indecisive mother a home, and nothing seemed to go right, we felt a lot better by saying a small prayer. At least it gave us a positive outlook when everything seemed pretty hopeless. I'm not sure if it helped open doors for us, but we seemed to find peace of mind in the process. Perhaps when you're trying your best for someone else's good, small miracles can happen if you open your heart and ask for help.

CHAPTER 5

Surviving the Hospital

A call for an emergency trip to the hospital is never a good omen, except maybe for the birth of a new baby. An emergency hospital trip is almost sure to result from a phone call at some predawn hour, or while you're beating a deadline at work, or packing for a vacation. You probably won't get the call to go to the hospital when you're sitting around with nothing to do.

My journey to the hospital for my elderly mom began with a call from the board and care home where she was staying. They informed me that she hadn't been eating well and now she was throwing up something with a foul odor. I met them at the emergency room of a busy hospital, the same busy hospital my dad died in six years earlier. When I arrived Mom looked tired, but rather thankful that I was finally there. We got her admitted through the emergency entrance, but the process took about four hours. Later, I found out that her own personal doctor refused to admit her himself – an act that could have simplified the admission process significantly.

Within a day they were running tests and sticking tubes in every orifice poor Mom had. Soon my sister and I were confronted with the results and the decision that had to be made. My mom's colon was blocked and infected. She was running a fever and growing weaker every hour. If she didn't have an operation, she would wither away and die. If she did have the operation, the chances of survival were only 50/50. There were no guarantees, and if she did survive, she would spend the rest of her life with a colostomy bag. What we learned from this hospital experience was that surviving this operation would be a difficult challenge for my mom, but surviving health care in a hospital today is an even greater challenge.

"...surviving health care in a hospital today is an even greater challenge."

While my mom was in the hospital, she was given a drug that she was allergic to (even though her allergy to the drug was written in her records when she was admitted), suffered a heart attack, and had a catheter improperly inserted in her that extended her bladder, causing an infection that hindered her healing process. She also developed bedsores within weeks of being admitted.

What I learned during the time Mom was in the hospital would change forever the way I would view hospitals. I always assumed that hospitals were safe, quiet places – refuges from ailments and injury, where a highly trained and caring staff looked after you. What I found out in this hospital stay was just the opposite. Hospitals today are treacherous places filled with well-meaning, but overworked, staff that make mistakes all too often. These mistakes are contained within the hospital itself and seldom reported to outside agencies. I'd like to share a few tips here that may help you avoid some of the pain these mistakes can cause you and your parent. From what others with elderly parents have told me, and from reports I've read in researching this book, I believe that accidents in hospital care are fairly common occurrences – especially with elderly patients.

"Hospitals today are treacherous places filled with well-meaning, but overworked, staff that make mistakes all too often."

As the child of an elderly parent, nothing is worse than the phone call you'll receive from the doctor or hospital informing you that your parent has fallen, had a stroke or a heart attack, has been rushed to the hospital, and you need to get there right away. Your mind may be going a hundred miles an hour and in a hundred different directions.

First, don't panic. You usually don't have time to anyway. Collect your parent's Power of Attorney for Health Care, the List of Allergic Drugs, and the List of Medications. Muster up your courage, and head out to the hospital. It may not hurt to say a little prayer on the way to calm down your emotions, then let your rational side take the lead. Hospitals are stressful places to visit. And there's nothing much worse than having someone you love in the hospital and in a situation that's often completely out of your control. But there are a few things you can do to take control during your parent's hospital visit. It's important to keep your emotional and mental state in control.

"As the child of an elderly parent, nothing is worse than the phone call you'll receive from the doctor or hospital informing you that your parent has fallen, had a stroke or even a heart attack, and has been rushed to the hospital, and you need to get there right away."

Getting Your Parent Admitted to the Hospital

Sometimes how your parent is admitted to the hospital determines if Medicare pays the hospital costs or not. If you have control over the admission process, you might want to make sure that either your parent's doctor has them admitted with a written order, or has called in the admission order ahead of their arrival. If their doctor won't have them admitted, as it was my mom's case, and the problem is acute, you'll have to admit them from the emergency room. Be very careful what you sign. You may end up getting a huge bill from the hospital or Medicare in the future. If your parent is unable to sign themselves in or you're worried that you'll be charged and feel you don't want to take on the responsibility, add the line "I'm only signing this so that my parent can be admitted to the hospital" before your signature. That's your "insurance policy" to help protect you from being held financially responsible. Help your parent fill out the admission forms. Make sure that everything is listed correctly and nothing important is omitted. Make sure the hospital knows what drugs your parent is allergic to and what pre-existing medical conditions your parent may have.

It's not taboo to come right out and ask if your parent's insurance or Medicare is going to pay for the hospital stay. It may put your mind to rest so you'll have one less thing to worry about.

If you haven't yet taken your parent to the hospital but know in advance that a hospital stay is looming, try and fill out the admittance papers ahead of time. You'll spare your parent the hardship of one more stressful thing to do during admission - filling out hundreds of forms. Being there for your parent during the hospital admission is one of the best things you can do for them, and it's probably what they would do for you.

What You Can Do to Help Prevent an Adverse Event

Once in the hospital, your parent will be involved in many procedures and tests, and you'll be on the sidelines, like a tired old supporter, offering encouragement and watching over them. Many things can go wrong in a hospital, and many of these things will be out of your control. In the rest of this chapter, I'll try to show you what you can do to take control of your parent's hospital stay, even if you have to work a day job, care for a family at home, and can only come to see your parent during visiting hours.

What is Medicare?

Medicare is a federal program that helps older or disabled people pay their medical bills. It's an entitlement program available to both the rich and the poor. Most U.S. citizens or residents of the United States for five years who are over 65 can qualify for enrollment. Those who aren't eligible for coverage may enroll and make monthly payments to receive coverage. Medicare usually pays for hospitalization and nursing home care for up to 60 consecutive days. Medicare comes in two parts:

● Part A is for hospital insurance and covers most of the costs of a stay in a hospital, as well as some follow-up costs after a stay in the hospital. To get Medicare to cover hospital care, you must be admitted by a doctor, or through the emergency room.

● Part B is medical insurance that pays for some doctor and outpatient medical care. Your parent is billed for the rest unless they have supplementary insurance. It usually pays for doctor expenses, exams, tests, ambulance rides to the hospital or nursing home, X-rays, hospital beds, wheelchairs, and the paraphernalia supplied by hospitals. It also offers some counseling by psychologists and social workers.

Medicare parts A and B don't pay all costs. You should make sure your parent has other insurance (usually called Medigap insurance) to pay costs not covered by Medicare.

In today's modern technological world we've come to expect better service from health care than most hospitals can deliver. Medical errors in hospitals have become frequent. Studies estimate that one million patients nationwide are injured by errors during hospital treatment each year. The number of deaths from hospital accidents is over 120,000 per year. That's about three times the number of people killed in automobile accidents each year. The sad news is that hospital mistakes aren't reported to the outside world. They're covered up within the hospitals themselves. Only recently have new laws been passed requiring hospitals to report their mistakes.

In a recent study, the Chicago-Kent College of Law determined that an "adverse event" took place during the hospital stay of 45.8% of the patients they researched. For nearly 18% of those patients, the adverse event was serious, with results ranging from temporary disability to death. The chance of a mistake increases as your parent's stay in the hospital increases. Your parent's chances for experiencing an adverse event increase by about 6% for each day they are in the hospital. Although surgery brought on about 10.5% of the adverse events in the study, most of the mistakes (28.3%) occurred during monitoring and daily care.

Ralph Nader determined that 300,000 to 600,000 people die every year because of medical incompetence. That would be like having casualties from 6 to 12 Vietnam wars every year in our own country. Yet, this is how many people die every year from doctor and hospital mistakes. I'm not bringing this up to scare you, but it's important to not be complacent while your parent is in the hospital. There are things you can do that will make a difference in how your parent gets through their hospital stay.

Just remember that hospitals are not safe places. Don't let down your guard and think that everything is under control. It's probably not. Here are a few things to watch out for.

Find Out the True Story of What's Going On

If your parent has already been admitted and you're just arriving at the hospital, ask to talk to the head nurse in charge of the floor your parent is on. You can try talking to other nurses, and if you're lucky, you'll find one who knows what the situation is, has the time to explain it to you, and can give you a vague prognosis on the outcome. From what I've seen in most hospitals today, nurses are overworked, underpaid, and not real eager sources of the overview that you're looking for. In fact, they'll usually feel as though the doctor is getting paid to bring that bit of information to you. So you may find the buck being passed to the doctor, who may not have had time to see your parent at this point. And you may not be able to find the doctor, as he's also very busy.

> "In a recent study, the Chicago-Kent College of Law determined that an "adverse event" took place during the hospital stay of 45.8% of the patients they researched. For nearly 18% of those patients, the adverse event was serious, with results ranging from temporary disability to death."

The head nurse is a good source of information. She'll usually be able to tell you what's going on. Be prepared to wait for her if you have to, because she's usually very busy. Give her your Power of Attorney for Health Care discussed in Chapter 3 and let her make a copy for her files. Present her with a list of medications that your parent is taking, and those that your parent is allergic to.

Sometimes the head nurse will only tell you so much and say that you have to wait for the doctor. In this case, the doctor will usually be your best source for the straight skinny on the problem. If either of them appears to be vague, or not telling you something, it may be because there's more to the problem than they want to get into, or they don't have any idea of what's going on. Either way, this isn't a good sign. Sometimes health care professionals are just not as helpful as you hope they will be when it comes to caring for elderly patients. If you're getting a smile and a vague prognosis on your parent, be insistent when you deal with health care personnel. Drill the doctor and the head nurse until you get the answers you need. Don't let them get the idea they're just dealing with another old person – let them know that this is your parent and you want answers that you can understand. You need straight answers on the problem and the outcome. Don't let them condescend or talk down to you. If they talk down to you, tell them about it. If necessary, bring in reinforcements – a platoon of concerned relatives demanding straight answers is more likely to get them.

"If you're getting a smile and a vague prognosis on your parent, be insistent when you deal with health care personnel."

Get to Know the Nurses

Try to get to know the nurses on a personal level. They have a difficult job caring for many patients while working long hard hours. They're the people who care for your parent when you're not there. They are the ones who usually detect a change in medical status in your parent when you're busy at work or at home with your family. Nurses often understand more about patients than doctors. They'll be the first to notice if your parent has an unusual reaction to some new drug that the doctor recommended. They'll usually be the first to catch sight of bedsores. You want to feel that the nurses are on your side, fighting against any unknown infection or surprise condition that can happen to your parent during their stay.

Unfortunately, chances are, you'll meet a new nurse every time you come in to see your parent. Make it your job to try and get to know all the nurses that take care of your parent. Some you'll probably like more than others. Try and think of them as your army, fighting for your parent's health. They're hard at work in the trenches, while you only appear in the evening or on weekends. Show them respect. Ask them politely if your parent can have more pain medication. Don't ever demand it like a buck sergeant. Be patient if they're busy and can't get to your parent right away. Remember, they have other patients to attend to. Even though it may be difficult, try and see the world through their eyes.

The Medical Chart

Every hospital keeps a chart on every patient. The chart monitors the progress of the patient and explains their vital signs on a kind of moving average. The problem with these charts is understanding them because every hospital uses a different type of charting system. Learning to read the hospital's chart is like deciphering a Rosetta stone for understanding what is going on with your parent. For example, many times you'll come in to see your parent and the nurses won't have time to really consult with you. In fact, you may not even see a nurse at all during the time you visit with your parent. But the chart tells all. You just have to figure out how to read it. Make an appointment with the head nurse and have her explain how to read the hospital's charts. Once you've conquered chart reading, you can go on to even bigger things – like trying to understand the doctor's handwriting.

Nurses are very knowledgeable about medicines. Ask them all the questions you need to. They usually won't feel that you're bothering them. In fact, they may feel flattered that you asked them. Sometimes it's a way you can get to know them.

Probably the worse thing you can do while your parent is in the hospital is to not become involved at all. Sometimes, when a loved one is in the hospital it becomes easy to detach oneself from the emotions and pain of the situation. Try not to let that happen to you, because if a situation comes up, and you could have prevented or stopped it, it will be you who suffers the guilt of knowing that later. Better to give it your best effort, even if that best effort is limited by what you know of medicine and by what you can control in a hospital setting.

Lend a Hand

Nurses generally appreciate any help you give them. If your parent needs their mouth swabbed out, ask them if you can do it. If the room needs a little tidying, go ahead and clean. If your parent needs some help with feeding, ask if you can help. There will probably be some things that the nurses won't want you helping with, but you'll always win brownie points for asking.

Speaking of brownie points, if your parent is in the hospital for a while, it probably won't hurt to bring in some cookies or a basket of fruit for the nursing staff to show them your appreciation. Especially if the cookies are homemade or the fruit is from your own trees. Try to make it a point to place a little basket of goodies at the nurses' station with every visit.

Have the Nurse Check the Catheter

A catheter is used to help a hospital patient urinate without getting up out of bed. As a visitor, you'll see it as a tube coming from a mystery spot under the sheets, and going into a bag filled with yellow liquid. Many times the catheter is improperly inserted into elderly women, causing an infection or an extended bladder, and a lot of pain. And sometimes no one will have the presence of mind to check the catheter insertion. Ask the nurse to check if it's properly inserted. This is one of the most common infection points in older female hospital patients. Yet, we must rely on the nurses to check it. An infection here can sap your parent's strength and delay recovery. It doesn't hurt or cost anything to ask the nurse to check. Stand by and make sure she does it while you're there.

Drug Allergy Notice

The patient _____ is allergic to the following types of drugs:

(1)_____

(2)_____

(3)_____

(4)_____

(5)_____

Therefore I request that you do not administer them.

These may include medications such as: (1)_____

(2)_____

(3)_____

(4)_____

(5)_____

(6)_____

(7)_____

Signed_____ Date _____

Relationship to patient _____

Figure 5-1 Drug Allergy Notice

Preventing a Drug Allergy Reaction

Post a copy of the Drug Allergy Notice Figure 5-1, at eye level, on the wall next to your parent's bed. The hospital will usually have all the information on your parent from their doctor's file – but that doesn't mean that all the nurses will take time to read this information. Nurses usually cycle from room to room on a three- or four-day basis. Every other time you come back to see your parent, you'll probably be explaining everything all over again to a new nurse. Allergic reactions to hospital-administered drugs can be life threatening to older people, and they do happen. It happened to my mom, and if we hadn't pointed it out to the nurse, she could have easily died – in fact, she nearly did. By posting this Drug Allergy Notice on the wall next to your parent's bed, you're doing your best to prevent the hospital from administering a drug that your parent is allergic to. Post it at eye-level to raise the odds that the nurse on duty will read it.

This form included on the disk in the back of this book.

89

How to Help Prevent Bedsores

If your parent is lying on their back in a hospital bed for a period of some time, there are certain parts of their body that will bear all the pressure of their weight. Typically these are elbows, heels, and the buttocks. Bedsores can start to develop here. Sometimes they even appear on the boney areas of the upper back and the back of the head. They develop where there's friction between your parent's body and the bed. After a while, the friction creates stress and inflammation. Bedsores are the scourge of hospitals. Once they develop, they're very difficult to heal, especially if they ulcerate. They weaken the immune system and make your parent more susceptible to other ailments. And they're not only demoralizing, they can actually become life threatening. They can also block your parent's return to a board and care facility. This means that if your parent develops bedsores and survives the hospital stay, they can only be released from the hospital to an expensive nursing home where licensed nurses are available to care for them. But there are ways of preventing bedsores from overcoming your parent.

Most hospitals require nurses to move a patient from side to side every so often so the weight of their body shifts and isn't supported by the same area. Sometimes this happens. Some hospitals offer electric beds that tilt back and forth like a boat rocking, in slow motion. You can request one of these beds.

But only you can really help to prevent bedsores. Every time you come to visit your parent in the hospital, check the heels of their feet. Are they soft and smooth? Or are they becoming red and callused on the heel area? If they are becoming red, or you notice a red spot forming that feels warmer than the surrounding skin, ask a nurse for sheepskin booties. These are little booties made of sheepskin that wrap around the heel of the foot to prevent constant grinding of the heel against the sheets of the bed. Every time you return to the hospital, check to make sure the booties are still on and haven't worked themselves off.

Check your parent's elbows. Gently lift them up and look for any red spots. Have the nurse help you check the buttocks. Usually, if your parent is lying on their back most of the time, their weight will be supported by their buttocks. Bedsores are the hardest to see here, and therefore the most likely to fester.

Checking for bedsores on each of your visits alerts the nursing staff that you're on the ball and checking up on your parent's care. They may be inclined to pay a little more attention to your parent. It also gives you a little job to do every time you come to visit. You can help by taking a little responsibility for your parent's health. Remember, the goal of your visits to the hospital is to offer support, sympathy, and encouragement to your parent that this is just a temporary stay. Don't stand there looking sad at them! Get involved and massage their feet and elbows!

"These are little booties made of sheepskin that wrap around the heel of the foot to prevent constant grinding of the heel against the sheets of the bed."

Bring a tube of lanolin or aloe ointment (available at nearly every drugstore) on your next visit and apply a small amount to your parent's heels and elbows. Work it in well. Try not to massage directly onto any red spots – just massage from the sides. Massaging is good, but if you rub directly onto a spot, it will only increase the friction. By sticking to a regimen of massage you can actually reverse the formation of many bedsores. At least you can keep them from getting worse and becoming an open wound. Your parent may also appreciate the attention. Many times when you find your parent incapacitated in a hospital bed, it's difficult to keep the conversation going. Seeing them in poor shape can make your mind lose track of witty or cheerful things to say. Working to keep the bedsores away gives you a mission. It also gives you a little feeling of control in what is pretty much an uncontrollable situation.

> ## Bedsores are classified by stages:
>
> 1. Stage one bedsores are red, tender spots that emit heat. If your parent's skin is dark you may not notice any redness, but you'll still be able to feel the heat. Stage one bedsores are still reversible with small amounts of lanolin, aloe vera, and gentle massaging of the skin around them.
>
> 2. Stage two bedsores are ones that have opened up and ulcerated. These are difficult to heal, even with antibiotics. They put a strain on the immune system, which is usually under stress to start with. Usually stage two bedsores require professional help and long periods of healing.

If your parent has been in the hospital long enough for you to worry about bedsores, you'll probably have made friends with a few nurses. Nurses will see your parent as someone with concerned family members. Hopefully, they'll pay a little more attention to your parent because they'll feel that you expect it of them.

Read Up on Your Parent's Diagnosed Situation

When you get home from the hospital, turn on your computer, fire up your Web browser and type your parent's ailment or predicament into a search engine. Start empowering yourself with knowledge on what you're up against. From this search you'll probably develop a list of questions to ask the doctor, and a string of potential outcomes. When the doctor asks you to make a decision regarding your parent's health care, your answer will probably be based on knowledge from this search and others like it in the days to follow.

How to Handle the Privacy Issue

If your parent is concerned about the lack of privacy in the hospital, post a large note like the one shown in Figure 5-2 asking all attendants to pull the curtain before giving an enema, inspection, or washing. Many times your parent may be sharing a room with another patient who has many visitors, and may want privacy during certain inspections or procedures. Post this notice at eye level in the room, near your parent's bed, next to the drug allergy notice.

This form included on the disk in the back of this book.

Personal Privacy Notice

The patient_____ would appreciate a certain amount of personal privacy and would like to request that the curtain be drawn when:

☐ Giving enemas

☐ Inspecting private areas

☐ Bathing or cleaning

☐ Using the bedpan

☐ Other _____

☐ Other _____

Signed_____ Date_____

Relationship to Patient:_____

Figure 5-2 Personal Privacy Notice

Surviving an Operation

Hardly anyone goes into a hospital these days without getting some kind of operation. If your parent needs an operation, here are a few things you can do to try to make sure they get the best care:

● Make sure up front that your parent's insurance or Medicare is going to pay for this operation. That way you won't be worrying about who is going to pay the bill along with worrying about the outcome of the operation. It will help you rid yourself of some extra stress.

● Make sure all lab tests were completed and checked over by the attending doctor before the date scheduled for surgery. To make sure, ask him or her a few questions about the tests. Act interested. As mentioned before, make it your role to ask lots of questions, and know something about the surgery by checking on it on the Web. Quiz the doctor until you get some solid answers. Make sure he knows he's operating on your parent and you care deeply about the outcome of the operation.

● Have a long talk with the surgeon and the anesthesiologist before the surgery. Find out exactly what they're planning to do. Ask them if the surgery is really necessary. Find out how many times in the past they have done this operation? What are the odds for a complete recovery? Get a clear understanding of what is going to happen. If they appear to field an answer, drill them until they give it to you straight.

● Ask about complications from the operation. Many older people are never the same after a major operation. Is there a risk of blood clots, delirium, or confusion to your parent from the operation? Again, try and get a straight answer. Don't accept a smile and an oblique answer. Don't let them get out of the room until they give it to you straight. Be prepared to be there for a while.

● Find out about post-operative care. Will your parent have to go to a nursing home? For how long? Will Medicare pay for it? What can you do to participate in the recovery process? How long should recovery take? What kind of drugs will your parent take and for how long? What are the side effects of these drugs?

● If you don't feel the operation is necessary, don't be afraid to get a second opinion. It may be that your aging parent won't be any better off even with the operation. In that case, you have to make a big decision, one that you'll want to take a "majority rules" vote on with your family members. An operation on an elderly person like your parent is always a major life event. Do everything in your power to be there during the operation and oversee it. Remember that hospitals aren't great places to be, so be there yourself to help your parent get through the event and out of the hospital as soon as possible. Be there to hold their hand when they are wheeled out of the operating room – even though they may be asleep.

Most operations will leave your parent dazed and confused. In fact, they may not be quite the same person as they were going into the operation. Don't expect them to start doing pushups or cartwheels any time soon after their operation. But don't give up on them either. Always, always, respect their dignity. Never talk about them as though they aren't there. Remember that even if they appear out of it, they can often hear you. Always be very careful what you say about them when you're within earshot, even if it appears they're sleeping. Give them the gift of your respect, and make sure that your family gets that message also.

Release from the Hospital

Sometimes older patients are released from the hospital to a nursing home. The nursing home should be a halfway house between the hospital and returning back to normal life. Sometimes the nursing home is the beginning of a new life of care. Once your parent is admitted to a nursing home, you may become involved with new therapies and new techniques for helping them. But if your parent has made it out of the hospital, you'll know that your prayers have been answered, for it usually means the crisis is over for now, and a period of convalescence is about to take place.

Take a few minutes to write a thank you letter to all the nurses and doctors who gave you or your parent special attention. They'll appreciate this positive reward, and it may affect the way they care for the next older person who is also someone's parent. Make sure you gather up all your parent's belongings from their hospital room before they're moved. Usually, your parent will be transported to a nursing home by an ambulance provided by the hospital. There's much more on nursing homes in Chapter 7.

> "But if your parent has made it out of the hospital, you'll know that your prayers have been answered, for it usually means the crisis is over and a period of convalescence is about to take place."

Dealing with Your Feelings

Nothing is much worse than the feelings you'll go through when your elderly parent goes into the hospital. Feelings of helplessness and despair can overcome you, especially if you watch them waste away in a hospital bed. And a lot of times, there's not a lot you can do, aside from quizzing the doctors, praying really hard, and massaging the bedsores away.

Instead of concentrating on what you could be doing for your parent, try and concentrate on what you *are* doing for them. Be proud of what you've done so far. Get together with your relatives and hold rallies of support over lunch or after visits. It helps to share your feelings and let out your insecurities. As you begin to talk freely amongst each other you'll notice that you're forming a tightly knit support group.

If you're feeling a lot of anger or resentment, try and find out where it's coming from. If it's blind rage, try and refine it by writing down your feelings. Getting a grip on things here can help you deal with your frustration, so you can grow stronger and overcome it.

If you're angry because a family member isn't helping or being supportive, try writing your feelings in a letter to that person. Then keep the letter in your word processor and change it as new things come up. You may even decide to print it out and read it. But keep it to yourself for now. As your parent is in the hospital, things can progress rather rapidly and everything may change in a matter of days.

The Power of Prayer

If you feel out of options, double-blind studies from several hospitals have actually shown that praying for patients seemed to help their recovery – but scientists can't figure out why. If you haven't tested prayer power by this stage of your life, and you've done everything else mentioned in this chapter, you might want to try praying for your parent's recovery.

If you are in the camp of people who don't believe in prayer, listed below are a few of the 191 studies that have determined that prayer has validity as a healing force. Many of the doctors who conducted the studies were skeptics themselves – until they saw the results:

A study was conducted by Dr. Randolph Byrd, a heart specialist at San Francisco General Hospital. This test was conducted on 393 patients who were admitted to the Cardiac Intensive-Care Unit. A computer chose the control group. To eliminate bias, none of the patients knew if they were being prayed for or not. Nor did the hospital staff. When the study was over, Dr. Byrd found that the prayed-for group were much less likely to develop congestive heart failure and pulmonary edema, and they were five times less likely to require antibiotics. The results of the "prayed for" group were statistically much better than the group which received no prayer.

Dr. William Harris and Dr. James O'Keefe at the Mid-America Heart Institute in Kansas City, Mo. conducted a double-blind test involving 1,000 heart patients that were admitted to the institute's critical care unit and secretly divided into two groups. The "prayed for" group had 11 percent fewer heart attacks, strokes, and life-threatening complications.

Dr. Elizabeth Targ, a psychiatrist at the Pacific College of Medicine in San Francisco has also tested prayer on AIDS patients. She found that the people who received prayer had six times fewer hospitalizations, and those hospitalizations were for much shorter periods, than those who received no prayer.

More studies on the effects of prayer on the sick are currently being conducted by researchers at Harvard University and Georgia University Medical Center. A large global study is now being conducted by Dr. Mitch Krucoff, a cardiologist at Duke University Medical Center in North Carolina.

The Spindrift Foundation in Salem Oregon have even conducted scientific tests on the effectiveness of various types of prayer. They tested "directed prayer" – for which there is a specific purpose in mind, verses "undirected prayer" – which is just for the best outcome for the person being prayed for. Their studies concluded that the non-directed prayers were three to four times more effective.

When your parent is in the hospital, you are limited in what you can do to help them recover and get out of there fast. But there are things you *can* do:

First, study their condition on the Internet. If there are alternatives to surgery or the elected course of action, discuss it with the doctor. Be proactive in their care. Make sure they don't receive treatment or drugs that affect them adversely. Watch for bedsores and massage their heels daily. And finally, if your parent is lying in a hospital bed, you want to make sure in the depths of your own conscience that you try to do all you can for them. If prayer can possibly increase their chances of survival by 11%, maybe it's worth a try.

CHAPTER 6

Dealing With Dementia and Other Mental Disorders

Dealing with dementia and mental disorders in your own parent can stretch the limits of your sanity. Sometimes you may not even notice the slow decline of your parent's memory until they start exhibiting signs of other mental disorders, such as paranoia or delusions, which frequently piggyback on the effects of dementia. These symptoms may keep reappearing, until you can't ignore them and you're forced to take some kind of action. Hopefully, this chapter will help you identify dementia and other mental problems in your parent and help you deal with the problem by getting their condition assessed by a professional.

My own mom taught school most of her life. She was highly organized and extremely independent. She read constantly and became quite adept at oil painting. At the age of 76 she moved closer to my sister and I, but her canvases and brushes never seemed to make it out of the moving boxes. I bought her a VCR for Christmas, hoping that renting movies could help her shake her newly-found disinterest in life. But the new VCR was never turned on unless I happened to visit with a movie in hand. It became, like the microwave I had gotten her a year earlier, another piece of unused technology. It never dawned on me at the time that my mom had stopped wanting to learn new things, or that this could mean that her mind was shutting down.

"Soon Mom became suspicious and paranoid about her neighbors."

Soon Mom became suspicious and paranoid about her neighbors. She thought they could see into her windows, so she would keep the shades drawn tight with safety pins. She talked me into erecting a large barrier to block the neighbor's view. I did as she asked, even though I thought it was strange to be building a barrier. Mom had always been a little paranoid anyway. I figured it was her scar from having survived the Great

Depression. I rationalized that if building a barrier helped her sleep better, and she could open the shades in those darkened rooms, it was worth the effort. I didn't realize the obvious – that her paranoia was growing.

Believing that Mom's depression was a result of her unhappiness with her living situation, my sister and I began our search to find her new housing. We placed our hopes on a retirement community that offered a full-time social director to rescue her from the depressed mood we were fighting. The retirement home helped her find new friends and subdued the paranoia, but only temporarily. Soon she insisted we change her banking accounts. She accused the banks of stealing money from her safety deposit box. She also became absurdly paranoid about my brother-in-law, who she suspected had a master key to her apartment. All missing items were blamed on this poor fellow.

The amazing part of all this is that my sister and I continued right on with our lives, denying Mom's odd behavior – while helping her change bank accounts and get new locks for her apartment. We just figured it was normal to become strange when you turn 80 years old. We never suspected dementia was taking her away from us.

"Symptoms of dementia are insidious, because they start so slowly."

Symptoms of dementia are insidious, because they start so slowly. Often they are mixed with periods of what appears to be normal behavior. So just when we thought she was going off the deep end, she'd return with what appeared to be complete clarity, asking us about our spouses and giving the usual motherly advice we had grown up with and trusted. Looking back, I can clearly see the progression of the disorder. But at the time, it sneaked in and stole Mom from us without a clue. Because of our busy schedules, hectic lives, and maybe a little denial, we didn't see it until it was too late.

There was also a strong fear going on. I remember thinking that if my mother was demented, I must be demented too. She was so close to me that I had a lot of her same thinking patterns. She dictated reality to me when I was growing up. I worried about this a lot. I really wanted her to be "normal" so I could feel normal. I didn't want anyone to find out my mom was acting crazy. I could just imagine everyone at work hearing the news and moving their fingers in circles around their ear saying "Ah ha! That explains it!"

"I remember thinking that if my mother was demented, I must be demented too."

So we took Mom to doctor after doctor trying to find a cure for her ailment. Was it low iron, low zinc, or low potassium? They drew countless pints of blood trying to rule out what could be causing her symptoms. But eventually, most of the doctors proved worthless in offering real help. Not one seemed to be able to tell us what was wrong. None of her five doctors could give us any advice that would help her. They all seemed to deny there was any problem. Fortunately, we met a geriatric counselor who advised us to take her to a local hospital for a geriatric evaluation. I wish we had done this evaluation five years earlier.

Identifying Dementia and Other Mental Problems

At the current time there is no real cure for the wide range of mental conditions classified as dementia. But here are some ways to determine if dementia is taking over your parent's life. If it is, there are steps you can take to slow its path, and keep your sanity in the process. Dementia opens the door for other mental conditions. Apparently, as the older brain compensates for the lack of memory, confusion, and other mental disorders, paranoia and delusion can move in. There are medications that can hold these disorders in check. But at this time, you can only slow the path of dementia. If your parent's doctors won't get involved, it may be up to you to notice that your parent has a problem and initiate action to treat their condition. The checklist in Figure 6-1 may help you identify any unusual behavior that may be warning signs of dementia or mental illness.

This form included on the disk in the back of this book.

Most Common Types of Dementia

While Alzheimer's disease accounts for the largest share of dementia cases (currently 50% - 60%), other forms of dementia also share in the battle for the mind. Lewey Bodies dementia is now in second place, accounting for 15% to 25% of all cases. Vascular dementia, otherwise known as multi-infarct dementia, ranks third.

You've probably already heard plenty about the dreaded Alzheimer's disease, or maybe you know someone whose parents have developed Alzheimer's. It is by far the most prevalent form of dementia, the most advertised, and usually presents the most severe symptoms. Most Alzheimer's patients develop the disease after age 70. At this time, nobody really knows what causes Alzheimer's disease.

Lewey Bodies dementia typically affects people between 60 to 80 years old. Males seem to be at the greatest risk. This disease comes on quickly, with episodes of delirium and prominent psychiatric episodes that include hallucinations. Sometimes there is difficulty with body movement, causing the patient to fall and lose consciousness. At one time, it was believed that this form of dementia was related to Parkinson's disease since the symptoms were similar.

Warning Signs of Dementia or Mental Illness

Everyone has unique traits in their personality. As your parent ages, these unique traits may grow stronger. You may eventually recognize that they have behavioral or social problems that need attention. Dementia may be at the core of these problems, but it may be masked by many other symptoms. No one is immune to memory lapses, moments of confusion, or misunderstandings. But there are some types of mental behavior that stand out and tell you it's time to do something. Some of these signs are:

❑ Your parent has stopped wanting to learn new things, such as how to use a computer, microwave, or VCR.

❑ Your parent complains that they are overdrawn at the bank and they suspect the bank is stealing their money.

❑ You come home to find your answering machine has a multitude of messages from your parent. It's obvious that each time your parent called, they forgot about the previous message.

❑ Your parent starts to tell your family members stories that are untrue. Or they "enhance" stories with a reality that differs from yours.

❑ Your parent repeatedly asks the same question, even though you've already given them the answer.

❑ Your parent complains about a neighbor and claims the neighbor is staring into their house or watching them. Or your parent is afraid of a neighbor for no good reason.

❑ Your parent's mood swings are out of control and they cry and laugh several times within an hour's time.

❑ You find that your parent's important bills have been paid more than once, or not at all.

❑ Your parent puts words in a sentence that don't belong, making the sentence difficult to understand.

❑ Your parent can't remember the names of your children, and makes attempts to cover it up. Or maybe your parent calls you or one of your family by another relative's name, and repeats this action again and again.

❑ You visit your parent's home and discover there are reminder notes all over the house. Some of them make no sense.

❑ Your parent continually buys more of what is already in the refrigerator because they forgot they already bought the items.

❑ The calendar has every day checked off and notes as to what happened on that day.

❑ Your parent has lost complete interest in a hobby or activity.

❑ When out for a walk with your parent, they rely on you to take the lead on the way back, as if they can't remember the way.

❑ You come to visit at supper time and they forget something cooking on the stove until you both smell it burning.

❑ Your parent can no longer even attempt to balance their checkbook.

❑ Your parent loses things and you eventually find them in ridiculous places.

If you've checked more than four of the symptoms above, you may want to get your parent to a doctor for an evaluation as soon as possible. Make sure you complete all of the legal preparations in Chapter 3 while your parent is still cognizant and coherent.

Figure 6-1 Warning Signs of Dementia or Mental Illness

Vascular dementia is caused by tiny strokes in the brain called infarctions. The symptoms are similar to Alzheimer's, but from what caregivers tell me, the symptoms aren't as severe as Alzheimer's. Afflicted patients have less tendency to wander than Alzheimer's patients, and may have fewer personality changes than Alzheimer's patients.

Many times dementia may be diagnosed as a combination of diseases. For instance my mom's dementia was diagnosed as caused by infarctions, which was determined by a CAT scan, but she also showed some indications of Alzheimer's disease. This diagnoses would imply that along with tiny strokes, there were plaques and tangles in her brain related to Alzheimer's disease.

While no single test can diagnose Alzheimer's disease, a trained physician can be 80-90% accurate. A clinical diagnosis of your parent's condition is really important, as it will tell you if the dementia is caused by reversible conditions, such as drug reactions, tumors, infections, thyroid problems, or nutritional deficiencies. Even if the dementia is diagnosed as irreversible, the diagnosis may identify other treatable problems that may be compounding your parent's dementia. And while there is no treatment today that can reverse dementia, you may be able to slow the deterioration it causes with drugs and vitamin supplements.

It's very typical to resist taking your parent for a clinical evaluation. You can tell yourself it will be too demanding for your parent, or too much hassle for you and your family. There's also the fear of knowing the worst. Knowing what takes place in the evaluation process at a geriatric evaluation clinic may help you overcome this anxiety.

Types of Dementia

The are many types of dementia, here is some information about some of them:

● Alzheimer's disease - Scientists are working on a vaccine, but currently there is no cure. Ibuprofen, Vitamin E , folate, and folic acid have shown some promise in preventing Alzheimer's, or at least slowing its path. Recent studies have shown that people who take at least 200 mg of Ibuprofen per day cut their chances of getting Alzheimer's by up to 50%.

● Vascular dementia - caused by strokes occurring in the brain. There are multi-infarct dementia, cortical micro-infarcts, lacunar dementia (large infarcts) Binswanger disease, and cerebral embolic disease.

● Anoxic dementia - caused by cardiac arrest, cardiac failure, and carbon monoxide.

● Traumatic dementia - caused by head trauma.

● Infectious dementia - caused by diseases such as AIDS or opportunistic infections such as Creutzfeldt-Jakob disease, herpes encephalitis, fungal meningitis, or parasitic encephalitis.

● Organic dementia - caused by brain tumors and cancer.

● Toxic dementia - caused by alcohol, mercury, arsenic, solvents, and even some insecticides.

Immediate Action to Take

If you start to notice odd behavior in your parent, make sure you've drawn up the important papers mentioned in Chapter 3; Power of Attorney for Health Care, Durable Power of Attorney, Life and Death Directives, and a good Living Trust.

Make the most of this time while your parent is cognizant of their life. Also, you have to realize that if they are losing it, the time for long meaningful talks will go by very quickly. If your parent has assets, and you haven't done so yet, consider taking them to a lawyer to plan their asset protection, as mentioned in Chapter 3. You want to be sure there will be assets available if your parent ends up in a nursing home.

The Doctor Visit

If you haven't done so by now, as mentioned in Chapter 2, get your parent to a doctor as part of a thorough physical examination. Normally, the doctor will take a blood test. One of the things he checks for is potassium level. Low potassium can affect memory and cognitive ability and make people act a little strange. Bring your prescription list from Chapter 2 to the doctor. The wrong balance of drugs can sometimes cause the brain to act strangely.

The blood test will also check for syphilis. I realize it seems absolutely ludicrous to think your elderly parent would have a venereal disease such as syphilis. But it must be completely ruled out before the doctor can go on to test for the next possible cause. The affects of syphilis on the brain over time can result in dementia-like behavior. Giving approval for the syphilis test is the start of the little indignities that will occur when your parent is suspected of having dementia. These indignities are the way older people with dementia are often treated by the medical community and the general public at large. You may find that it's difficult for anyone to show genuine compassion for them and their condition.

Memory Field Test

To test for dementia a doctor can perform a memory field test. The doctor will explain to your parent how he will make the test. During a casual conversation, he will list three items that your parent should try to remember. In my mom's case, it was a red Cadillac, Elvis, and a birthday cake. Then he'll engage your parent in some other conversation and ask them a few difficult questions such as "Who is the current President of the U.S.A?" or "Who is the Vice-President?" After this distraction, he'll ask your parent to repeat those three key items (red Cadillac, Elvis, and a birthday cake) he mentioned earlier. If your parent fails to remember two of the three, the doctor will probably recommend further testing at a hospital that tests geriatric patients for memory and mental problems. If he doesn't recommend further testing, be sure to ask him why he doesn't.

CAT Scan

Sometimes, if your parent fails the field test, the doctor may recommend a CAT scan to find any undetected strokes that may be causing the abnormalities in their behavior. If your doctor doesn't recommend this, ask about it. A CAT scan can see through layers in your parent's brain and search for an undetected stroke. Recent studies have found that silent, small strokes may be present in as many as 80% of people with dementia. If your parent has high blood pressure, this is especially applicable, as their arteries may harden with age and small pieces may break off and cause tiny clots in the vein. These micro strokes in the brain are called infarctions. They can short-circuit the brain's wiring, causing dementia. While you can't undo the damage of these strokes, you can see that your parent takes the correct drugs to help prevent future strokes – and, hopefully, slow your parent's mental decline.

Dealing with Doctor Denial

After Mom failed the field test for dementia, the doctor rolled his eyes and put his palms out as if to say, "What do we do now?" He took us aside and told us Mom was just getting old and maybe a little forgetful – nothing to worry about. I wish we hadn't accepted this answer. If you know in your own mind that your parent's memory problems are getting worse, you may have to take the initiative yourself. Unfortunately, to the doctor, your parent may be just another old person that's losing their memory but is still able to cope. Since there is no cure for dementia, the doctor may not be willing to deal with something he can't prescribe a pill for, or thinks he can't help heal. Or maybe it's a communication gap between doctors and caregivers. In a recent survey conducted by the Alzheimer's Association, it was discovered that over half of caregivers wanted to know how Alzheimer's would affect their patient's ability to do normal tasks, but only 28% were able to get this information from their doctors.

"After Mom failed the field test for dementia, the doctor rolled his eyes and put his palms out as if to say, "What do we do now?"

How to Find Screening

Get out the Eldercare Directory. You can usually find these little gems at your local senior center, or you can check their Web page at www.eldercare.com. If you can't locate a resource guide, call the senior center and ask them if they know of a local hospital that does free screening by geriatric specialists. If they don't know, call a local hospital directly and ask for the number of a geriatric assessment center. If you live in the U.S., there are usually at least two hospitals within 30 miles of you. One of them should know of a geriatric assessment center near you. Try calling the Alzheimer's Association Helpline at (703) 359-4440 or the National Association of Geriatric Care Managers at (520) 881-8008. Don't give up. Don't deny to yourself that your parent has a problem. Your parent may themselves notice that something strange is going on in their behavior. But they may blame that behavior on something else — such as being overly tired or hungry. Or they may blame their medications.

The Geriatric Assessment Evaluation

If your parent is on Medicare, the test at the geriatric assessment center is free. You may find it important to get your family members involved before you take your parent for evaluation. Later, if guilt sets in for being the one to take action, you'll have someone to share it with, and someone to remind you that you had no other choice. The hospital evaluation for dementia can be a real turning point in your parent's life, and your life as well. Usually, your parent will be required to spend several days in a hospital while undergoing physical and psychiatric tests, and evaluation by a medical and psychiatric team who specialize in geriatric disorders. The team will assess your parent's condition, prescribe drugs, and help you plan for your parent's future care.

"Leaving your parent in a geriatric hospital for two days won't be easy for you either."

The downside of the test is your parent may feel they are just fine and don't need to go to any hospital for testing. They may also not want to face the fact that they're losing their memory and their grip on life. Most elderly people enjoy their independence and don't want to think about being mentally incompetent or dependent on another person for care. They may be very reluctant to find out the truth of their condition. Be gentle, and remind them that it's what the doctor wants. A phrase that worked for me was "Let's get it over with so you can feel better." And "Let's get a professional evaluation so you can feel better."

Leaving your parent in a geriatric hospital for two days won't be easy for you either. It wasn't easy for me. If you're not careful, guilt will begin to torment you. If you think it over carefully, you'll realize that what you did, had to be done. Find someone you can talk to comfortably. Perhaps you can discuss it with a good friend of your parent – someone who can back you up and go with you and your parent to the evaluation center.

Talk with other family members too. This whole episode, though one of great pain and tribulation, is a great opportunity to get to know your family better. It can bring you all together and make your family stronger. Don't cheat any family member out of the chance to share emotions or memories with you during this episode in your parent's experience. Pull out your Family Agreement Form from Chapter 1. This is the time to enforce it. Turn this misfortune into an opportunity to bond with your family. If you have a family member who isn't ready to help, move on to the next one. Don't hate them if they're unable to join in to help your parent. You don't know everything going on in their life. This is a painful part of your journey through life – an opportunity for understanding and love. If your family doesn't have the love, time, or understanding within them to help your parent, forgive them and move on. Some day they'll probably regret their decision, and you can talk about it then. But right now, you need allies, friends, and support.

Once your parent gets to the hospital or testing facility, they'll probably enjoy the attention and all the questioning they receive from the staff. They may even enjoy the time they spend in the center – especially if they're currently living alone and have few people to talk to.

The Actual Exam

While your parent is in the hospital they'll be diagnosed by a trained staff of around five people, who will give them an interview, test, and physical examination that includes blood tests to rule out all curable causes for dementia. Then they'll probably give your parent a neurological examination and laboratory tests such as an electroencephalogram to record activity in the brain, a CT scan to make an X-ray of the brain, or an MRI scan to produce a picture of the brain.

After these examinations, they'll probably administer a series of psychiatric evaluations to make sure that your parent isn't suffering from depression or another psychiatric ailment that mimics the symptoms of dementia. They'll perform psychometric tests to determine your parent's area of impairment and areas of remaining strength. They'll also test your parent's abilities to perform routine tasks necessary for taking care of themselves.

The staff will check the prescription and non-prescription drugs your parent is taking, especially the ones that can affect the central nervous system. Be sure and bring your parent's drug list you prepared in Chapter 2.

Eventually they'll have enough data to diagnose your parent. If it's found that your parent has controllable mental disorders, they'll prescribe a cornucopia of psychotropic drugs in an attempt to achieve normalcy. These drugs should help your parent cope with the frustrations of losing their memory, and the side effects of memory loss, such as hallucinations and paranoia. This will help your parent enjoy more of the time they have left in their lives.

Sometimes, as in my mom's case, in the search for the appropriate drug dosage, the doctors will start high and gradually decrease the dosage. When you visit your parent at the clinic, they may be on an emotional roller coaster ride that will continue until the doctors find the correct drug dosage to return your parent to as normal a state as possible. A few months after your parent is discharged from the geriatric evaluation, you may find that these drugs have caused your parent to mellow considerably. In fact, you may want to cut back on the dosage before they mellow into a vegetable. If your parent starts to fall asleep constantly in front of the TV,

> "If your family doesn't have the love, time, or understanding within them to help your parent, forgive them and move on. Some day they'll probably regret their decision, and you can talk about it then. But right now, you need allies, friends, and support."

What Causes Mental and Memory Disorders in Older People?

According to the National Institute on Aging, there are actually around 100 conditions that can cause serious memory and mental problems in older people. Most, if treated, are reversible. Others, such as degenerative diseases, can't be reversed. Here are a few examples:

● Reactions to medications: Older people taking more than one prescription – especially mixing sedatives, hypnotics, neuroleptics, anti-hypertensives, and anti-arthritic medications can cause side effects that may seem like a mental disorder.

● Emotional distress: Depression or major life changes such as retirement, divorce, or loss of a loved one can affect one's physical and mental health. Depression can also show up as memory loss. Be sure and inform the doctor if your parent has experienced any emotionally-stressful events recently.

● Metabolic disturbances: Renal failure, liver failure, an increase in anti-diuretic hormone, hypoglycemia, hepatic diseases, or pancreatic disorders can provoke a confused state of mind and bring on changes in sleep, appetite, and emotions.

● Vision and hearing: Problems seeing or hearing may be perceived as dementia in older people because the person isn't able to perceive surroundings or understand conversations.

● Nutritional deficiencies: Inadequate folic acid, niacin, riboflavin, thiamine, vitamin B-12, potassium, and zinc can cause cognitive impairment. If your parent has been living

(continued on page 107)

don't hesitate to call the doctor back and discuss cutting the dosage. You'll probably have to take charge here, because when your parent is released from the geriatric assessment center, you'll become your parent's advocate. They'll be relying on your care and judgment from this point on.

Learning to Live With the Stigma

Degenerative brain disorders may cast up a whole host of horrible images. Visit a few Alzheimer's nursing homes and you'll quickly understand why. It's very scary to be around people who appear crazy. But just because your parent has a memory problem doesn't mean they have full-blown Alzheimer's disease. If they do have Alzheimer's, it doesn't mean you're going to get it. The stigma of Alzheimer's is so strong that sometimes you may not even want to face the fact that your parent may have it. You may just pretend your parent has a little memory problem. The only problem with this is that your parent's memory just seems to get worse. Left untreated, the problem grows, causing confusion, misunderstandings, and paranoia. Some day you may get a call from the police saying they found your parent wandering around lost in a busy intersection, in their underwear. Or your parent may take their nest egg money out of the bank and hide it somewhere and forget where they put it, as my mom did, or accuse someone of stealing it. You don't want things to come to this point, so overcome your fears. You've got to take action – and quickly. You've got a parent who needs your help.

If your parent is actually diagnosed by the hospital as having dementia, it's time for you to get busy planning for the future. You'll probably feel confused, and have a sense of loss, like your parent has died, and yet is still living. Rest assured, they'll come back now and then for short spells. But the time for long discussions and analysis of complex problems with them is probably nearing an end.

You may also feel instantly stigmatized, as if a family weakness dwells within you. You may find yourself wanting to keep it secret. Every time you have a memory lapse you'll fear you have caught the dementia yourself. But try not to worry – studies have shown that if your parent has late onset Alzheimer's, (the most common form that develops after age 65) your chances of it passing on to you when you reach age 65 are only around 10%. However, this chance will rise another 10% if your brother or sister also gets it.

"Every time you have a memory lapse you'll feel as though you have caught the dementia yourself."

Support Groups

This may be a good time to consider joining a support group to meet other children of parents with dementia. Their stories may make you feel much better. You can learn how others managed to make it through their crises and survive. When you talk with others who have parents with dementia, their stories will usually relate how dementia has affected their family. Sometimes just sharing these stories can create a few laughs, and maybe even a few tears. A good support group will help you realize that others share a similar pain and frustration, and there may even be a few horror stories worse than yours.

While trying to find housing for my mom, I visited an old friend who shared the stories of his mom doing somersaults in her underpants to get the attention of an elderly man at her nursing home. The hilarious episodes he'd been through made me realize two important things:

1) No matter how bad things look - they always look funnier when they happen to someone else and:

2) A sense of humor can get you through practically every difficult time in your life.

What Causes Mental and Memory Disorders in Older People? (continued)

alone and their eating habits haven't been nutritionally sound, this could be a cause. Have their doctor recommend a personal diet to fit their health problems and nutritional needs.

● Endocrine abnormalities: Hypothyroidism, parathyroid disturbances, or adrenal abnormalities can cause confusion that may seem like dementia.

● Infections: Older people can develop infections that bring on sudden states of confusion. Once recognized, this can be easily treated and often completely cured.

● Blood clot on the brain: Draining the fluid before it can cause permanent damage can treat these clots.

● Hardening of the arteries: This can also cause dementia as a series of tiny strokes occur within the brain. If treated early enough, the patient can be helped. If not, the symptoms are similar to Alzheimer's – though not as severe.

● Degenerative diseases: These are diseases that cause irreversible brain damage. The most common is Alzheimer's disease. Other diseases that can cause dementia are Parkinson's disease, Huntington's disease, and multiple sclerosis.

● Brain tumors: These growths can cause mental deterioration. Sometimes they can be removed surgically.

● Spinal fluid build-up: When the flow of spinal fluid is interrupted and not absorbed properly, it builds up inside the brain and creates pressure. The symptoms may seem like a mental disturbance.

Advanced Housing Needs

This is probably a good time to sell your parent's car, and arrange for a move to a facility as mentioned in Chapter 4. If your parent has been living alone for some time they may actually enjoy the move, as they'll be with other people at their own level. At least they won't have to cook for themselves any more, or be stressed trying to remember if they took their pills. Try and find a facility that matches your parent with other people of the same age and level of comprehension. In other words, don't move them into a locked Alzheimer's clinic if all they need at this time is a little care, such as having their meals prepared and transportation provided. Normally, at the beginning stages of dementia, they can move either to a residential care facility or a large institutional care facility, as mentioned in Chapter 4.

Try to find a place that fits your parent's current needs, while keeping one eye on the future. Before long they'll need more intense care. Some facilities, and even some residential care facilities, have a three-step program offering these levels of care:

1. A ward of a large care facility or a residential home that offers a trained staff, transportation, prepared meals, social contact, and a private or semi-private room.

2. A ward of a facility or residential home that offers a trained staff and/or nurses, supervised transportation with a group, medicines administered by the staff, help with bathing, prepared meals, social activities, and a private or semi-private room.

3. A ward of a facility or residential home that offers a trained staff and/or nurses, transportation supervised with a group, medicines administered by the staff, help with bathing, hygiene, diapers, prepared meals, help with eating, social activities, and a private or semi-private room.

In this type of facility, as the need for care grows, more care is available. The monthly bill for the facility grows as the amount of care grows. Scout out both large care facilities and the smaller residential care facilities to see which ones are the best for your parent's needs. You can use the checklists in Chapter 4. You may want to try having your parent stay in a large retirement facility and see how they do. You may consider moving to a smaller residential care facility when they need more care. A residential care facility can usually provide more care for less money than a larger facility that has more overhead to support.

When my mom was released from the assessment center, the doctors said she could not return to her retirement home and that she needed to be in a facility providing 24-hour care. My sister and I had one weekend to find that facility. Moving Mom from the assessment center to her new home wasn't easy – especially when she wanted to go home, but couldn't quite remember where home was. We just kept telling her that she had to stay in the new place a little longer. It was only a few days before she forgot her old friends and her old surroundings. I'm sure she felt better, but it took longer for us to get over our feelings of having betrayed her.

Dealing With the Decline

Current tests are checking to see if Ibuprofen, Vitamin E, folate, and folic acid can help slow the slide into deeper stages of dementia. Also, gingko biloba taken twice a day may improve mental conditions, at least it has helped prevent the tiny strokes that cause infarctions in the brain. Ibuprofen has been shown to help prevent the inflammation that leads to Alzheimer's. Your parent's doctor may also try a few of their miracle drugs such as tacrine (Cognex) and donepezil (Ariept). But don't expect any turnarounds, because these drugs seldom do much more than slow the inevitable decline.

You can also work at trying to get your parent to use their brain more. You've probably heard the phrase, "Use it or lose it." That phrase has been clinically proven in cases of dementia. Use crossword puzzles or TV quiz shows to try and get your parent to think and use their memory. Encourage your parent to use and exercise their brain. But be very patient with them. Go slowly. Again, don't expect miracles; they don't happen very often. Pushing too hard will just cause frustration. You probably aren't going to be able to stop the decline anyway. There is no cure for dementia yet. But if you work hard at it, you just might be able to slow the decline enough to get in a few more good heart-to-heart discussions.

"There is no cure for dementia yet. But if you work hard at it, you just might be able to slow the decline enough to get in a few more good heart-to-heart discussions."

Communicating During Your Parent's Decline

As time goes on, your parent may be more removed from reality. Trying to bring them back is a losing battle. After a while you'll realize it's best to just go along with them. Don't argue or get mad or disappointed. If they claim someone is leaving uneaten sandwiches in their refrigerator, go along with them. You're not going to be able to change their reality. You'll only make them, and yourself, more depressed.

There's a new skill you'll learn to change the way you interact with your parent. It's referred to as re-direction. Re-direction is a way of taking control of the conversation. When you talk with your parent, instead of asking them a question they have to think about to give you a reply, start off with a positive statement that only needs an easy response. Take control of the conversation. At first it will feel very awkward, especially if your parent was the one always challenging you mentally.

Communicating With Your Parent Who Has Dementia

1. Turn down the television or move your parent to a spot away from competing noises.

2. Always begin your conversation with eye contact. Identify yourself and call to them by name.

3. Speak slowly in a low-pitched voice and maintain an open, calm, and friendly manner.

4. Avoid sentences phrased in the negative. Instead of saying "Don't go outside, say, "Stay inside."

5. Avoid open-ended questions. Offer a yes or no answer, or a choice between two items.

6. If your question wasn't understood, rephrase it slowly with a smile and a little love.

7. Give plenty of time for your question to be answered. It will take them more time to process questions now.

8. Never interrupt them when they're talking. They may lose their train of thought.

9. Don't argue or contradict your parent. Go along with them, no matter how silly it may seem. If it's real to them, let it be.

10. Don't try to get your parent to remember things they have forgotten. Encourage them to talk about familiar places, interests, or past experiences they can remember.

11. Show your parent you love them. A smile and a hug can go a long way in communicating.

12. If you're stumped as to what to talk about, take them for a walk or a drive. The most important thing is that you're there, and you show them that you love them.

But after a while you can become really proficient at it. When your conversation lags with your parent and you're both staring at each other, take the helm and start re-directing the conversation. Watch how the staff of your parent's care facility does it. They've become experts at this form of communication. And they're usually pretty good teachers too.

As time goes on, usually 2 to ten years after diagnosis, your parent will probably be moving to the next level of care. They may still be able to eat without help. But they'll need to be reminded of mealtimes and gently coaxed to the table. They'll need some help with bathing and personal grooming. They'll probably need to have someone monitor their bowel functions. They won't be as talkative as they used to be, and they might have trouble forming the words that once came easily. Sometimes they may make up stories. They may hear or see things that aren't there. By now you'll have been paying the bills and have control of the checkbook and finances. And hopefully you'll have them in a care facility where they have 24-hour care. They won't recognize old familiar places and may even have trouble recognizing your children. Don't let it break your heart. Accept it. Help your children accept it. Let the sadness wash over you. Grandma may not remember your children, but she can still accept their hugs and love.

If your parent keeps asking when dinner time is, you may want to place a sign written in large clear letters saying "Dinner is at 5:00 p.m." to remove anxiety about something they have to remember.

You may find that certain repetitive actions are signals you can read. Pulling at clothing or shuffling of the feet may be a sign that your parent has to use the bathroom.

Wandering

No one seems to know what causes wandering or the restlessness that brings it on. Maybe wanderers are bored and looking for adventure. But wandering can be dangerous if the wanderer can't figure out how to make it back home. In most residential homes or care facilities there is an electronic device that will emit a piercing beeping sound if the door is opened by someone other than the caregiver. These devices tend to discourage wandering. If your parent wants to walk, see if you can go with them. It will probably do you both some good to go on a walk together.

Incontinence

This starts when your parent can't seem to remember where the bathroom is. Finally, after enough mistakes, it's easier to put them into adult diapers. But you can start by asking your parent approximately every two hours if they have to go to the bathroom. Limit their intake of fluids during the evening hours. Use illustrated signs to indicate where they can find the bathroom. Place these signs in all the rooms. Make sure they wear clothes that have elastic waistbands and are easy to remove so they can get them off easily.

Angry or Agitated Behavior

Usually there are drugs that can calm down most dementia patients who display angry or agitated behavior. Sometimes avoiding coffee or stimulants helps. Generally, residential care facilities won't take your parent if they display angry or agitated behavior. In fact, sometimes the only place that will take them will be a large institutional-type facility with muscular orderlies and huge monthly bills.

There are some things you can do to reduce angry and agitated behavior. Eliminate the clutter in their room and try to keep familiar objects at hand, such as photographs or objects that evoke pleasant memories. If your parent appears agitated, try a gentle touch, soothing music, or take them for a walk. Instead of asking what they would like, say something like "Hey Mom, let's go for a walk." If your parent is restless at night, try leaving a light on in their room. Acknowledge your parent's anger over the loss of control in their life. Tell them that you understand their frustration. Then distract them with an activity of some kind. Let them forget about the troubling incident. They don't have the skills to confront troubling incidences anymore – best you let them forget it and move on.

Dealing With Wandering

1. You can get child-safe plastic doorknob covers in many hardware stores. Special electronic devices that can be turned on or off are very effective also. These electronic devices emit a loud piercing beeping noise when a door is opened.

2. Have your parent wear identification at all times. Keep a current photo of them in case you may have to report them missing.

3. Inform your parent's neighbors of your parent's wandering behavior and make sure they have your phone number.

4. Make sure your parent gets enough daily exercise so they're less likely to get restless and want to wander.

"Acknowledge your parent's anger over the loss of control in their life. Tell them that you understand their frustration. Then distract them with an activity of some kind. Let them forget about the troubling incident. They don't have the skills to confront troubling incidences anymore -- best you let them forget it and move on."

Terminal or End Stage Dementia

The next stage, which is called the terminal stage, lasts from one to three years. This is where the locked doors prevail to prevent wandering. At this stage, your parent will need help in dressing, bathing, and feeding. Their muscles may twitch and jerk uncontrollably. They may not recognize you, or even themselves in the mirror. They may pull at invisible strings, moan, or make grunting noises. By now their bowels and bladder are beyond their command.

"Once in a while, during this stage, the parent you knew may come back, as if they have just been staying somewhere else, far away from their body. They will tell you something they feel is important, and talk to you with complete clarity."

At this time you'll feel a sense of loss that is difficult to describe. Once in a while, during this stage, the parent you knew may come back, as if they have just been staying somewhere else, far away from their body. They'll tell you something they feel is important, and talk to you with complete clarity. In one such session, my mom did exactly that. She told me she wanted to make it perfectly clear she never wanted to go back to the hospital again. Listen carefully if you see them struggling to share something with you. It may be important. It may be one of the last times you can talk with them about anything. Dementia may be the hardest road for you to follow your parent down. When the end stages of dementia appear, you are full of both sadness and anticipation – sadness because you realize that it will soon be time to say good-bye, and anticipation because, given the life your parent currently is leading, you may believe they will be going to a better place.

The first sign of the end stages of dementia appears when your parent no longer wants to eat. They may have trouble swallowing. They may have trouble speaking, and when they do speak, their words may be only gibberish. Or they may speak clearly but so softly you can't understand what they say. Some dementia patients forget how to swallow correctly, so they inhale food or drink. They may even lose control of their throat muscles to such a degree that it will appear they've eaten or drunk something and start coughing. It isn't long before their lungs fill up and they develop pneumonia. At this point they may have also lost the ability to walk. They'll probably be in diapers by this time, as they usually also become incontinent. And one morning at the breakfast table they'll just start refusing to eat or drink. Their teeth will clench and they'll refuse to let in any food or water. Then you'll know the end will be arriving soon. It isn't that they don't like the food you're offering – it's that they sense it's time and they just don't want to eat anymore. Or maybe they're just not getting the signal that their body wants food anymore.

Participating in the effects of end-stage dementia with your parent is so difficult for a caretaker or child, that when they finally die, you're actually happy for them. They're finally in a better place. And you can't blame them for not wanting to live when you understand the quality of life they have left. It may also be surprising to find that you have few tears left to shed. Perhaps you already shed all you have. You already said your good-byes long ago, when they were there to respond in some way.

After they pass on, you may find that you have a very short mourning period because you'll come to realize that you've been in mourning for a long, long time, but you didn't know it until now.

To have a parent die from dementia affects your life profoundly, but in subtle ways that are difficult to explain. You may find yourself wondering about your purpose in life. You may find that the career you've had for so long is a sham, or pales in comparison with the experience you've been through with your parent. You may want to stop and smell the roses when you're already late for work. You may start to wonder about your own quality of life and take steps to improve it. One thing remains certain, something in your life will change. It's almost as if God rewards you for the experience by giving you new eyes to see the world. Those new eyes will see your day-to-day life in a whole new light.

> "After they pass on you may find that you have a very short mourning period, because, you'll come to realize, that you've been in mourning for a long, long time, but you didn't know it until now."

As painful as this experience may be, you may find that it offers you a gift. The experience of losing your parent to dementia or mental disorder may give you an opportunity to become a more spiritual person. Maybe this is a way of coping with the chaos of what has happened to your life and the life of your parent through this tragedy. You may find solace in seeking a higher source for some kind of understanding of what is happening when nothing seems to make sense. And in this process sometimes something beautiful can happen within you.

If your parent has been diagnosed with dementia, you may feel angry, frustrated, and even ashamed. You may be overwhelmed with the choices you now have to make in short order. One thing that worked for my sister and me was to pray for help. Neither my sister nor I was particularly religious at the time, but we both felt it offered a great sense of comfort – especially when we had to make an important decision or when we felt overwhelmed. One such prayer that may help is the Alcoholics Anonymous Serenity Prayer which goes:

Prayer for Serenity

God grant me the serenity to accept the things I cannot change, courage to change things I can, and wisdom to know the difference.

Notes

_____

_____

_____

_____

_____

_____

_____

_____

_____

_____

_____

_____

_____

_____

_____

_____

_____

_____

_____

_____

_____

_____

_____

_____

_____

_____

_____

_____

_____

_____

CHAPTER 7

Nursing Homes

When you think of a nursing home you probably think back to a time when you visited your grandma, or when you, as part of a volunteer group, went to sing Christmas carols for the residents. But nursing homes aren't always pleasant places to visit. They can conjure up unhappy images of awkward visits to some ailing older person in a wheel chair muttering incoherent words, or howling like some type of monkey. But according to surveys from actual nursing home residents, those images exist mostly in our minds as visitors to a home. Many older people actually enjoy their stay in a nursing home. This may be because of the attention they receive while at the home, or maybe because they find companionship with others their own age in the same predicament.

"Many older people actually enjoy their stay in a nursing home."

More than 40% of people over age 65 will stay in a nursing home at some time in their life. For some it will be an extended stay, and for others it will be just a temporary stay while recuperating from trauma or an operation.

My mom was referred to a nursing home straight from a hospital. Since my sister and I were ignorant about which home to send her to, the hospital made the choice for us. Looking back, I don't think that it was the best choice. The nursing staff didn't speak English well and conversed to each other in a foreign language. Sometimes, when we would ask for something, they would speak to each other in this language and laugh. At times, because of the language barrier, I was never quite sure what they were saying, even when they were trying to explain something relating to Mom's condition. I'm sure they got tired of me asking them to repeat their words over and over. Also there was the smell of dirty diapers. The odor seemed to have worked its way into the ventilation system.

When Your Parent May Need a Nursing Home:

1. Your parent is released from the hospital and needs help with recovery that you are unable to provide. This may include speech therapy, occupational therapy for personal grooming, help with eating, and physical therapy for walking and movement.

2. Your parent's doctor has determined that their medical condition needs full-time skilled nursing care.

3. Your parent's condition is too much for the family to handle at home and home health care services are too expensive.

4. Your parent develops mental conditions such as dementia or psychosis, requiring full-time care.

5. Your parent can't care for themselves or maintain their own personal hygiene (bathing, dressing, bathroom activities, or brushing their hair or teeth) as a result of illness, injury, or psychiatric problems.

6. Your parent decides they need more attention, interaction, and companionship than what can they can get at home and has the means to pay for nursing home care.

"They usually have a regimen of exercise, good nutrition, and therapy to help your parent get back on their feet."

Luckily, my mom was there only a short time. While there, she recuperated from emergency surgery for a plugged colon. In the nursing home, she learned how to speak, swallow, and care for herself again. Although she was never the same after the surgery, the nursing home helped her get back on her feet. Soon she was well enough to return to the residential board and care facility she lived in before the operation.

For me, it was very difficult to see Mom in a nursing home. And not just because the quality of her life was suffering, but also because I knew that from this point on, I would be taking a more active role in her welfare and her finances. Nursing homes are expensive. When your parent lands in a nursing home, they'll need your help in ways you may not have considered before, as well as your active participation in the choices in their life. This chapter will tell you what you can do to provide that help and make those important choices.

What Nursing Homes Do

Nursing homes are primarily designed to give high-maintenance care for people recovering from illness or operations. They also provide long-term nursing supervision for people with chronic medical problems. A nursing home isn't a hospital, and can't provide surgical care for acute conditions as a hospital can. The goal of a nursing home is to provide therapeutic care and treatment to return a patient to their highest possible level of physical, mental, and social well-being. After a major operation, your parent may be discharged from the hospital directly to a nursing home. If your parent has been admitted to a hospital via the emergency room, or under a doctor's orders, they'll usually have 100 days in a nursing home for convalescence that will be paid for by Medicare.

Nursing homes offer special care from qualified, trained nurses and visiting therapists. They usually have a regimen of exercise, good nutrition, and therapy to help your parent get back on their feet. Their job is to push your parent back on the road to recovery. By the time your parent gets to a nursing home, they may be tired of living, and unable to care for themselves. The nursing home staff is highly aware of this. Their job, as they usually see it, is to get your parent back to where they can take care of themselves. Part of that job is to motivate your parent towards recovery, so they can once again lead an ordinary and fulfilling life without help from nurses.

Judging a Nursing Home

To protect patients, all states require some form of licensing for nursing homes. State inspectors regularly visit nursing homes to make sure they comply with state laws and Medicare and Medicaid regulations. Those licensing requirements help ensure that nursing homes today are well regulated and subject to regular state inspections. It may be difficult to find a really bad nursing home, but your goal should be to find the best nursing home for the money – the one that best fits your parent's needs for an affordable price. At this point, probably the worst thing you can do is to pay for more, or less, care than your parent needs. You'll want to find the type of nursing care that's just right for your parent.

What Are the Main Medical Reasons for Going to a Nursing Home?

- Alzheimer's disease
- hip or other serious fracture
- heart or circulation problems
- senility
- stroke
- confusion and forgetfulness
- no main medical condition – family cannot provide care for them

Types of Nursing Homes

Here is information on three types of nursing homes. I've included acronyms for the different types. Nursing homes often use these acronyms when they refer to themselves, so it's a good idea to remember them when you go to check out the homes.

Intermediate Care Facility (ICF) – provides only 8 hours of care a day. These facilities do not always have licensed nurses available. They provide medical, intermittent nursing, dietary, pharmacy, and activity services.

Skilled Nursing Facility (SNF) – provides 24-hour care and nursing supervision by registered or licensed vocational nurses. These facilities provide long- or short-term health care and assistance with many aspects of daily living. They also provide speech, occupational, and other therapy a patient needs for daily living.

Skilled Nursing Facility Severe Disabilities (SNFSD) – provides 24-hour care for people with severe mental disabilities. Many of these facilities have locked or secure living areas for the patients' protection and the protection of others.

Shop Around

When a hospital has to send your parent to a nursing home, they'll consider your insurance options and ask you to pick a nursing home covered by your parent's insurance plan, or by Medicare. Usually the hospital will ask you to choose a nursing home; otherwise they'll pick one from their list of favorites. These favorites may be nursing homes they receive special favors or kick-backs from. As I found out, they may not be the best place for your parent. Before your parent is discharged from the hospital, get to work to find a good nursing home right away. Don't simply accept the nursing home referrals the hospital gives you. Follow the guidelines listed in the section below to find the best nursing home for the money. While bargains in nursing homes are few, you can find big differences in the care offered by homes within the same price range. You just have to shop around.

Finding a Good Nursing Home

Look in the Yellow Pages of your phone book, your local Eldercare directory, or visit the local senior center for a list of nursing homes. A few great Web sites to check are www.seniorcare.com and www.NursingHomeReports.com. They both issue reports, for a small fee, of nursing homes within driving distance of your home. These reports list how the state inspector graded the homes, based on cleanliness and other inspection factors. Also try www.medicare.gov for the latest scoop on complaints filed against nursing homes.

This form included on the disk in the back of this book.

Whatever you do, don't ever judge a nursing home by the size of their ad in a publication or newspaper. Plan on devoting a few mornings for reconnaissance visits. Make a list of nursing homes by location, get out your map and make a route so you can inspect a few each time. Use the Nursing Home Evaluation Checklist shown in Figure 7-1.

The Reconnaissance Tour

You should be able to walk about freely in most nursing homes. I recommend taking a reconnaissance tour for your initial impressions, either by yourself, or, if you can arrange it, with another family member. As you walk through a nursing home, unannounced and on your own, try to imagine that you have been admitted as a 90-year-old patient. Ask yourself how you feel about the home. Would you be comfortable there while convalescing from a fall, stroke, or major operation? Follow the list of questions in Figure 7-1. So you don't forget any particular aspect, print out the checklist and take it with you on the tour.

Nursing Home Evaluation Checklist

Name of home _____

Type of home _____

Address _____

City/State/Zip _____ Phone _____

Monthly cost _____

Environment

	Yes	No	Somewhat
Is the location good?	❑	❑	❑
Is there adequate parking?	❑	❑	❑
Does it smell good?	❑	❑	❑
Is the environment comfortable?	❑	❑	❑
Do the residents seem happy?	❑	❑	❑
Are the residents well-dressed and clean?	❑	❑	❑
Are the individual rooms bright and cheery?	❑	❑	❑

Comments: _____

_____

Staff

	Yes	No	Somewhat
Does the staff speak good English?	❑	❑	❑
Are they respectful of the residents?	❑	❑	❑
Do they have a sense of humor?	❑	❑	❑
Do they offer assistance quickly?	❑	❑	❑
Do you see any doctors?	❑	❑	❑
Can you trust the orderlies?	❑	❑	❑

Comments: _____

_____

Figure 7-1 Nursing Home Evaluation Checklist

Nursing Home Evaluation Checklist (continued)

Meals	Yes	No	Somewhat
Are meals served at regular hours?	❑	❑	❑
Is the central dining area kept clean?	❑	❑	❑
Is there a menu?	❑	❑	❑
Can residents eat in their rooms?	❑	❑	❑
Is there assistance with eating?	❑	❑	❑
Is assistance with eating handled well?	❑	❑	❑
Are special dietary needs accommodated?	❑	❑	❑

Notes: _____

Access	Yes	No	Somewhat
Can you visit any time?	❑	❑	❑
Is there a private area for visiting?	❑	❑	❑
Can you take your parent outside?	❑	❑	❑
Are there phones in the rooms?	❑	❑	❑
Are there trips to the mall or library?	❑	❑	❑

Notes: _____

Activities	Yes	No	Somewhat
Is there an appointed activity director?	❑	❑	❑
Do the activities seem upbeat?	❑	❑	❑
Do activities cost extra?	❑	❑	❑
Do activities include crafts and games?	❑	❑	❑
Are there activities during weekends or eves?	❑	❑	❑
Are residents encouraged to participate?	❑	❑	❑
Is there a space in the facility for activities?	❑	❑	❑
Can residents continue in their own hobbies?	❑	❑	❑

Notes: _____

Figure 7-1 Nursing Home Evaluation Checklist (page 2)

Nursing Home Evaluation Checklist (continued)

Privacy	Yes	No	Somewhat
Does staff respect the privacy of patients	❑	❑	❑
Does staff knock on the door before entering?	❑	❑	❑
Can a resident bathe or shower anytime?	❑	❑	❑

Notes: _____

Personal	Yes	No	Somewhat
Do clothes come back from the laundry?	❑	❑	❑
Can residents have personal belongings?	❑	❑	❑
Can residents receive newspapers or magazines?	❑	❑	❑
Do they have a policy on missing valuables?	❑	❑	❑

Notes: _____

Medications	Yes	No	Somewhat
Does a nurse administer daily medications?	❑	❑	❑
Can residents keep non-prescription drugs?	❑	❑	❑
Can your parent keep their own doctor?	❑	❑	❑
Is medical support is available in emergencies?	❑	❑	❑

Notes: _____

Services	Yes	No	Somewhat
Is a hair salon or personal grooming available?	❑	❑	❑
Is day-to-day dental service offered?	❑	❑	❑

Notes: _____

Services	Yes	No	Somewhat
Is there someone to call when you have questions?	❑	❑	❑
Is your parent's care reviewed regularly?	❑	❑	❑
Will you be involved in the review?	❑	❑	❑

Figure 7-1 Nursing Home Evaluation Checklist (page 3)

Nursing Home Evaluation Checklist (continued)

Overall impression of facility:

❑ excellent ❑ good ❑ fair ❑ poor

Notes:_____

_____

_____

_____

Figure 7-1 Nursing Home Evaluation Checklist (page 4)

After conducting your initial reconnaissance tour you may want to take the official tour. Though nursing homes may look the same on the outside, you're looking for the subtle things that can identify the exceptional from the usual.

Let the staff, or the marketing manager of the home, give you the complete tour package. Look for the unseen. Here are nine things to look for:

1. As you walk in the front door and wander the halls, let your nose be your guide. What do you smell? Is it feces and urine, or is it bleach, vinegar, or Pinesol? Does it smell clean or is it putrid? If you smell dirty diapers, mark that on your checklist. This smell can tell you that while the staff may be good, they may be spread too thin to give your parent the type of care you're looking for. That smell may indicate that patients aren't having their diapers changed regularly or soiled garments aren't disposed of properly. You don't want your parent or yourself in an environment that smells bad.

2. Does the staff speak English as a second language? We import from other countries nurses to fill low-paying nursing jobs in nursing homes. While they may be competent caregivers and possess compassion and gentleness, the day may come when you'll need to communicate a problem and find that no one truly understands you. They'll smile and nod, but you'll see that a chasm exists in your communication with the staff that hold your parent's life in their hands.

3. Are there activities planned for the patients throughout the day? Are there daily activities and entertainment, or are patients left to sleep and watch TV in their rooms? Do you see the patients in wheelchairs corralled in a big room watching live entertainment or special shows to increase socialization?

4. Do the residents and their families seem happy in their environment? How do the residents appear to you? Are they wandering around aimlessly? Do they

appear to be under the influence of sedatives? Do you see any residents tied to their wheelchair or bed? Restrained patients may also indicate a lack of staff. If you can muster up your courage, take one of the residents aside and ask them what they think of the place. Make sure you're out of earshot of the nurses or orderlies. Sometimes you can get the real lowdown this way. It may surprise you that these residents may be happy to share with you what they think. In fact, they may be flattered you asked. Also be aware that an unhappy camper at one of these places may delight in making up horror stories for shock value.

5. Meet the orderlies. These are the people who are really in the trenches. Do they appear content in their work? Do they look like someone you'd feel comfortable leaving your parent with? Or do they look like tattooed gang members? If someone is going to take advantage of your parent while they're in a nursing home, chances are it will be someone in this bunch. They are the lowest paid and hardest-worked employees.

Do they look like someone you'd feel comfortable leaving your parent with? Or do they look like tattooed gang members?

6. Check out the noon meal if you get a chance. You'll see firsthand how the orderlies help the residents . Do they have a caring relationship with the residents or are they simply shoveling food down their throat? Do they have a sense of humor? Is there a dining area where residents can socialize? Are the patients socializing within their ability?

7. In case of a medical emergency, is a doctor available at all times, either on staff or on call? Do you see any doctors in the facility? Can your parent keep their own doctor, or do they have to use a doctor from the facility who you do not know?

8. What kind of day-to-day dental care is available? Is there some kind of care for brushing, flossing, and denture cleaning? Or do you have to pay extra for this?

9. Are call buttons located near each bed and in the bathroom? Do they work? Are there fire sprinklers? Are there phones in the residents' rooms?

The State Inspection Report

If you find a nursing home you like and you think your parent would approve too, ask for the Inspection Report from the Health Care Financing Administration. This is the final X-ray inspection into violations that may have been committed and found during inspection. Look for the violations that affect residents, such as over-restraints or unhealthy kitchen procedures. The staff may give you dirty looks and develop a haughty attitude when you ask for this report, but don't let this faze you. You want the best for your parent. And if the home is really good, you shouldn't be made to feel bad for wanting to look a little deeper to see if it's truly as great as it seems. If they won't show you the report, maybe you should continue your search.

Once you've made your choice, bring your parent there (if you're able to) and explain to them why you like this home. It's best if they approve of your decision. If they disagree, try not to get angry. Explain to them patiently how much time you spent on research trying to make the best choice, and why you decided on the one you did. Most of the time, your parent won't be in a position to be involved in the process of choosing a nursing home. The decision-making process may be entirely yours and your family's.

Making Your Parent Comfortable

Once you settle on the nursing home, you'll meet with the administrator and sign the papers. If your parent is able to come with you, take them around and introduce them to the residents and the nurses. If your parent is already in the hospital, you and a family member will probably have to go through this process without them. The ambulance will move your parent from the hospital to the nursing home after all the papers are signed.

If your parent is moving from a hospital or other facility, it's best to be at the nursing home when they arrive, even if you have to take off work or find someone to babysit the kids. *It's important to be there for reassurance.* Take some photos and other items your parent is familiar with and place them around the room so your parent feels at home. Bring their bathrobe, slippers, and some comfortable shoes for them. Find out from the staff what your parent may need. Be sure to use a permanent marker to write your parent's name on all their clothing. Clothing can get mixed up in the laundry.

"Keep in mind that when your parent is in a nursing home, it's probably a good time to have that heart-to-heart talk you've been putting off."

Visit Frequently

Once your parent is settled, try to visit at least twice a week. Stagger the visits among family members so you don't all appear on one night, and your parent is alone for the next several nights. Bring the kids. Just about all the people in a nursing home enjoy seeing youngsters. Let your parent brag about their grandchildren to the other patients. If you can't visit often, use the telephone. Keep in mind that when your parent is in a nursing home, it's probably a good time to have that heart-to-heart talk you've been putting off. This is the time to tell them how much you love them, and maybe even that you're praying for their recovery. Tell them how much you care for them. This is the time to tell them everything, as if maybe there's no tomorrow.

Get to Know the Nurses

A nursing home is a lot like a hospital, only not nearly as chaotic. But like a hospital, it pays to get to know the nurses that watch over your parent. Establish a rapport with them. Bring them home-baked cookies, brownies, or fruit from your trees as mentioned in the chapter on Surviving the Hospital. Ask about your parent's progress. Show concern. The nurses will usually respond to your caring, and remember you and your parent. If you remain special in their memory, they'll be more likely to call you when things don't look good, and give you a progress report with a smile when things are going well.

"Bring them home-baked cookies, brownies, or fruit from your trees."

Having a good relationship with the nurses will help when you have a concern or notice a problem that needs attention. If you notice something that isn't right, it's usually best to deal directly with the person responsible (like the orderly who hasn't changed a wet diaper on your parent), rather than going over their head. Mention your concern to them in a way that shows respect for their job (you realize that they are busy) but also indicates concern for your parent. Keep the problem between you and the person who caused it unless you notice it happening again. Then bring it up with the head nurse. Mention that you have already had a talk with the orderly, or person responsible, about it.

Handling Major Problems and Concerns

If you feel there's a big problem, for example, your parent is being ignored or placed in isolation and their physical and emotional needs aren't being met, ask for a meeting with the head nurse to find out what's going on. There are usually two sides to every story. If you aren't satisfied, take charge and have your parent moved to another nursing home.

If the problem is major, you can always contact the National Citizen's Coalition for Nursing Home Reform at 202-332-2275. They can guide you through the problem and help you take appropriate action.

Attending Assessment Meetings

Usually nursing homes hold assessment meetings on the progress of their patients. The staff and therapists meet to discuss how your parent's rehabilitation is progressing. It's an important meeting that you should be part of. Try to have at least one family member there with you also. Be punctual and don't be afraid to ask plenty of questions. Remember, these administrators and therapists are paid for by your parent's savings or insurance or by taxpayer dollars. Don't be intimidated by their advanced degrees or healthcare language. Get your money's worth by asking them every question about your parent that you can think of. Make sure that by the time you leave the assessment meeting, you've gained a good understanding of your parent's condition and where they can go from here. Don't be afraid to ask if your parent will soon be eligible to reside in a less-expensive care facility. In other words,

Assessment Meeting Questions

Is my parent making good progress on their recovery?

Are there complications that you haven't told me about?

If so, what were these caused by?

Are the therapies bringing about the desired results?

Is there something I can do to help?

How much longer will my parent require this therapy?

When can my parent return home or go to a care facility offering greater independence?

How much care will my parent require when therapy is completed?

Figure 7-2 Assessment Meeting Questions

will the therapy enable them to be more independent in the future, and if so, when? Figure 7-2 has a list of potential questions to bring up at an assessment meeting.

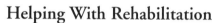

This form included on the disk in the back of this book.

Helping With Rehabilitation

Nursing homes typically give your parent therapy to try and bring them back to self-running mode. They'll give speech therapy to get your parent speaking and swallowing again. They'll give occupational therapy to teach your parent to groom themselves and brush their teeth again. They'll give physical therapy to help your parent develop muscles to get them moving around again. These therapists usually want your input. Make sure you talk with them directly. If you can't meet them at the nursing home, call them. Find out what they're doing with your parent, and what progress is being made. Your parent and their therapist will appreciate your interest and concern. You may be able to fill in some answers on your parent's case that the therapist may need to know – background information that can help them with your parent's therapy. Also, the therapist may have you help your parent with the recuperation process.

Handling Nursing Home Expenses

Nursing home care is fairly expensive. Prices range from $20,000 to $50,000 a year. Medicare will pay for some nursing home care (usually the first 100 days) if certain medical requirements are met. You may have to prepare yourself to kiss your parent's nest egg (and your inheritance) good-bye if their stay is long-term and not covered by their insurance. Unfortunately, most people never plan to enter a nursing home and don't prepare for long-term health care ahead of time.

Long-term Insurance

If your parent has long-term insurance, they've done their homework and they're in good shape financially. Alert the Nursing Home Administrator and most of your parent's financial worries will be taken care of. For the rest of us – who thought that it would never come to this – there are ways of affording long-term care within your parent's means. You just have to think creatively, weigh the options, and make some hard choices. Not many people carry long-term insurance. Most long-term insurance premiums get more expensive as the insured person gets older. Some insurance companies have even been known to levy large increases in their premiums as policyholders reach the age at which the policy might be used. If your parent doesn't have an extremely large nest egg to spend on a nursing home (over $500,000) and doesn't have a long-term insurance policy, you'll need to start thinking creatively about ways of financing your parent's stay.

Sources of Financing

Take a look at your parent's finances on their Personal Financial Worksheet in Chapter 3. Try and figure some safe ways you can make these assets generate enough income to help pay for your parent's stay in a nursing home. If they have a home that's paid for, consider renting it to generate income, instead of selling it. This way you, or someone you hire, can manage it by renting to produce income without touching the principal value of the home. Calculate if the rental income generated from their house, along with pension, dividends, social security, and interest income from their nest egg savings, can get them through the door of a nursing home. If you can use the rental income from your parents home to generate income to fund their stay, you may not have to sell the home – which means you'll be able to keep it as part of their assets. The key is to have it generate income.

If they have a car, it's a good possibility they may not need it any more. Discuss this with them and then, if necessary, sell it. Advertise it as driven by a little old lady and charge a premium price. You'll probably get it. Tell the buyer that you're using it to help fund your parent's stay in a nursing home. If the buyer tries to get you down in price –– introduce him to your parent and make him feel like a heel. Don't laugh. This technique worked for me!

Typical Nursing Home Scenario

A typical scenario could go like this. Your mother has a fall and fractures her hip. She is admitted to the hospital via the emergency room, and Medicare covers the hospital visit. She survives the hospital but is unable to return home since she's confined to a wheelchair and can't care for herself. The doctor recommends a nursing home. The ambulance takes her there and you meet to sign the admission papers. Medicare will pay for 100 days of recovery care. After that the costs can soar to $4,000 per month, plus incidentals (drugs, haircuts, etc.). Your mother has been living on a small pension and Social Security benefits of around $2,000 per month. If she has a home, you'll have to sell it, or rent it out and manage the rental. If she has assets, you'll have to deplete them on a monthly basis, until she has only $2,000 left (if she has no spouse). That's when Medicaid kicks in and foots the bill. Medicaid is the safety net for those who have no assets of their own to fall back on.

Medicaid first looks at your parent's income. For an individual or an individual with an ineligible spouse, the maximum they can make is $1,536 per month. For a couple, the maximum is $3,072. Medicaid counts everything you make as income: Social Security benefits, veteran's benefits, pension benefits, interest or dividends, royalties, rental income, civil service annuities, railroad benefit, state retirement benefits, gifts, and earnings or wages.

Next, Medicaid looks at your parent's assets. These include: money in the bank, certificates of deposits, IRA's, property, life insurance policies, stocks and bonds, jewelry and antiques, cars, tractors, and vehicles – basically everything that's worth anything. The most an individual can have before collecting Medicaid is $2,000 in assets. Couples are allowed to have $3,072.

However, your parent is allowed to hold on to a few things. They may have a homestead they intend to return to someday, life insurance worth less than $1,500, burial funds worth $1,500, a car, provided it's worth less than $4,500 and is used for medical transportation, and a burial plot.

(Continued on next page)

Asset Protection

If you want to protect your parent's assets there are many ways to do so. However asset protection is getting tougher all the time. Getting your parent to go along with your schemes to protect their assets may be difficult also. Here are a few ideas to get the "asset preservation" part of your mind working:

● If your parent owns a house, enters a nursing home, runs out of money and must eventually turn to Medicaid to finance their continued stay, Medicaid can, after they die, take the house for payments owed. To avoid this, your parent can quit claim the house to you, or, if they have one, the executor of their Trust. Remember the Living Trust that you set up in Chapter 3? The executor should be the one responsible for managing the house as a rental for income.

● When your parent runs out of money and applies for Medicaid, the government will search through their bank records to see if they ever had any money that suddenly disappeared from their accounts. They'll take Deep Throat's advice and "follow the money." If they find out that your parent "hid" the money to be eligible for Medicaid, they'll penalize. One way to avoid this penalty is for your parent to give their money to their children every year for several years before entering a nursing home. Then they should keep only enough for the first six months in a nursing home (around $30,000). After the penalty period is over, Medicaid will continue to pay for their nursing home care. The $30,000 allows them to stay in a nursing home for at least six months, which is usually the period necessary before Medicaid starts to pay.

● If your parent's spouse is alive, the rules are different. Your best money here may be spent on a visit to a financial advisor and a lawyer to help you start a plan. The rules on nursing home and Medicaid eligibility vary from state to state, and seem to change from year to year depending on which political party is in office. The money you spend on a financial advisor or lawyer who specializes in asset protection can save a large part of your inheritance in the end. Ultimately however, the real choice is your parent's. They may not feel comfortable being on the dole. Even though you may feel distraught about watching your inheritance go down the drain, you must ultimately follow your parent's wishes. But a trip to a lawyer specializing in asset protection – even if you pay for it yourself – will make you and your parent aware of the options available.

Visiting an Asset Protection Lawyer

Call your local bar association – usually located in the Yellow Pages of your phone book, and ask for a lawyer that specializes in asset protection. The first visit to a lawyer is usually free when you are referred by the bar association. Get the most from this visit by writing down all your questions ahead of time. Here are some things to bring to the meeting:

1. your living trust

2. your parent's asset worksheet

3. a plan for the future (subject to change)

4. a notepad and pen

5. a family member

> ## Typical Nursing Home Scenario (continued)
>
> Sometimes, if your parent has a house that is generating rental income, they'll be allowed to keep it. Sometimes, if a certificate of deposit is generating income that will help pay medical bills, Medicaid will view it as an income source rather than a lump sum. Income sources usually don't have to be liquidated to pay for care. To be sure, consult with an attorney specializing in asset protection to make sure of the rules involving income-generating assets.
>
> If your parent has a spouse, the couple is allowed to keep $84,120 as protected assets (not including the $4,500 car and the burial plot).
>
> But if your parent is single, all they may keep is a homestead they intend to return to someday, life insurance worth less than $1,500, burial funds worth $1,500, a car, provided it's worth less than $4,500 and is used for medical transportation, and a burial plot.

The lawyer will recommend choices you can make to protect your parent's assets. Write down these choices – they can help you formulate a plan of action. Eventually, the lawyer will try to talk you into his services. Ask him point blank what he'll charge. If he waffles, tell him you need a ballpark estimate. Then thank him and leave. You can always come back. Dealing with lawyers is sometimes like dealing with used car salesmen. Sometimes it's better to leave and come back later, when your emotions aren't in overdrive, than to rush into action. You might want to make this first visit just a fact-finding mission. Before you leave the lawyer's office, ask him if he can refer you to a good financial planner he is used to working with. Many lawyers who work in asset protection partner with financial planners as team members to help their clients.

Visiting a Financial Planner

Many people calling themselves financial planners are just using the words "financial planner" to gain your confidence so they can sell you something you don't need – such as stocks or high-commission mutual funds. That's the last type of person you and your parent need to meet right now. Most states require certification for financial planners. To receive this certification they have to pass a set of rigorous tests. Some financial planners also specialize in helping elderly people. You can usually find them by referral from asset-protection lawyers. You can also find financial planners in the Yellow Pages of the phone book. Before you visit a financial planner, ask for references. Call those references and make sure they are elderly people whose lives were changed for the better by the financial planner and his services.

Bring the same things you brought to the lawyer's office to the financial planner:

1. your living trust

2. your parent's asset worksheet

3. a plan for the future (subject to change)

4. a notepad and pen

5. a family member

A good financial planner may suggest ideas that you never considered. They've had years of experience making money stretch for elderly people. Hopefully they'll come up with ideas you may not have thought of. However, these ideas come at a price. That's how financial planners make their living. Most certified financial planners are free agents who work for themselves, so their fees are often negotiable. Don't be afraid to tell them that what they are planning to charge for their services is more than your parent can afford! This tactic may get you a better price and show your parent you're looking after their best interests. At least it will show your parent that you're capable of bargaining in their behalf.

Another thing to consider with a potential financial planner is whether you and your parent can get along with them. Sometimes, bringing up the subject of their fee has a way of exposing the real person. With a financial planner, you are looking for someone knowledgeable, but also someone you can trust and get along with.

Moral Options to Consider

If your parent doesn't have long-term insurance and doesn't want to take the financial planner's or lawyer's advice to protect their assets, try not to despair over any loss of inheritance. Remember, your parent's money belongs to your parent. They earned it, and they saved it. Even though you may have had plans to buy a red Mercedes convertible with your inheritance (to help you overcome the grief of your parent's death, of course), you have no right to your parent's money. You are in the driver's seat of a trust-mobile. Your parent trusts you to help take care of their life.

And now that you're in the driver's seat, it doesn't hurt to remind yourself that this is an opportunity to prove to yourself that you're a good person. It may be that God is watching you. At least your family members will be watching you. Sometimes you'll have to make difficult choices and your decisions may depend on your own set of morals. Many of these will seem like thankless tasks. Try and keep the highest standards for your decisions, so that no one, and especially yourself, will ever question your integrity. Once you have gathered all the facts surrounding a decision, try to consult with your family and bring them into the decision-making process.

> "Remember, your parent's money belongs to your parent. They earned it, and they saved it. Even though you may have had plans to buy a red Mercedes convertible with your inheritance (to help you overcome the grief of your parent's death, of course), you have no right to your parent's money."

Nursing Home Alternatives

You may want to consider the options listed below for alternative care that's not as expensive as nursing home care. Someone once said "You can't always get what you want. But if you try, you may get what you need."

At-Home Nurses

At-home nurses will come to your house, or your parent's house, and give one-on-one care, either part-time or full-time. If there is a non-skilled family member who can be with your parent most of the time in their home, this may also be a viable option. If you or your parent has a spare room, and you can gain the support of your family on this decision, it might be worth a try.

Pros: Your parent receives quality care in a familiar environment.

Cons: requires full time care by a combination of family members and caregiver. Lacks social interaction of other people your parent's age offered by a nursing home. Occupational and speech therapy will cost extra.

Cost: $500 to $4,000 per month

Religious Nursing Homes

You may find less-expensive nursing home care provided by certain church organizations. And your parent doesn't necessarily need to be a member of that church to be accepted. Besides offering excellent care at an affordable price, these organizations usually offer a religious focus, nourishment for the soul, and may be more interested in doing good than making money off your parent. You may appreciate this when approaching all the trials and tribulations of nursing home care. You'll usually find that the staff and administrators are honest and helpful.

Pros: Nursing home care with emphasis on religious teachings and a belief in the soul.

Cons: Not suited for everyone, especially those who aren't deeply religious. Facilities may not be the most modern.

Costs: $1,000 to $4,500 per month.

Residential Care Facilities

If your parent is admitted to a nursing home for intensive after-hospital convalescence and therapy, they may be well enough after a few months to be admitted to a residential care facility. As mentioned in Chapter 4, these facilities operate out of private homes. They don't have a 24-hour nursing staff, but they do have trained caregivers who reside at the facility. They can usually arrange for a nurse to visit twice a week, and they can arrange trips to the doctor on an as-needed basis. They usually provide a family-type setting and offer residents their own or a shared room. Your parent would join the other residents for meals and activities. Residential care facilities cost considerably less than nursing homes. If your parent doesn't require 24-hour nursing care they shouldn't have to pay for it, especially if they can't afford it.

Pros: Affordable care in a family-like setting with fewer residents.

Cons: May not fill required medical needs. Cannot take patients with open bedsores, and other conditions, based on state-mandated rules. Does not provide 24-hour nursing care.

Costs: $1,500 to $3,500.

Assisted Living Facilities

Also mentioned in Chapter 4, these facilities have nurses on staff, but they may be located in another part of the facility and available only on a when-needed basis. So while the nurses are nearby and capable of providing 24-hour care, your parent doesn't pay for them until they are needed. These facilities may cost less than a nursing home, depending on the level of care required.

Assisted living facilities are usually in large, institutional-type buildings. They may provide care at three levels. The first level may be just a retirement facility providing a small apartment with meals and activities. The second level may provide assisted living with all the services of the first level and additional assistance with medications, bathing, and other everyday living necessities. The third level may provide all of the services of the first and second levels, plus additional nursing care.

Pros: Your parent is paying only for the level of care they need, which can be upgraded without them having to move to another nursing home.

Cons: They may be operated by large profit-driven organizations that can nickel and dime you with extra charges for trips to the doctor, dentist, hairstylist, therapist, etc.

Costs: $2,500 to $4,500 per month.

Don't Expect an Overnight Cure

When your elderly parent suffers a stroke, fractures a hip, or suffers a mishap that results in a stay in a nursing home, it may take a while before you begin to notice any improvement. Older people improve much more slowly than you may expect. Don't expect quick cures or fixes. It's not likely to happen. Sometimes it may take up to six months before you begin to see improvement in your elderly parent's condition, but don't give up hope. They usually do improve, even though they may complain to you about the treatment they're receiving, the food they're forced to eat, and the therapy they have to go through. But the moment you leave the front door of the nursing home, they may be back in the social room having a good time.

It's not easy watching the one who took care of you much of your life age and end up in a nursing home. You may feel guilty that you're not spending enough time with your parent – especially when you're trying to juggle your time between a career and a family. You may also get a deep-down feeling that your parent's time is running out. That's when it's very important to make the most of your visits. Remind your parent that you love them and care for them, and that you're there to help them get better.

"You may also get a deep-down feeling that your parent's time is running out. That's when it's very important to make the most of your visits. "

Nursing homes are meant for rehabilitation – they make very expensive and depressing retirement homes. The more you can encourage and help your parent in the rehabilitation process, the faster they'll get on the road to recovery. Much of the recovery process may evolve around a positive mental attitude in both yourself and your parent. This positive attitude may be a little difficult to evoke in both of you at a time like this. You may consider joining a support group if the nursing home offers it, or you might want to gather support from your family members.

Sometimes, an event like your parent entering a nursing home can serve as a catalyst to unite family members who may have not worked well together until this crisis made it necessary. You may be surprised to find a positive family experience arising from this whole event. Try to build on that positive emotion so that your parent is aware of it. And it can help you through practically any sadness.

It's never easy to see the parent who raised you confined to a nursing home. But if you work hard you might just be able to encourage them to make this a pit-stop for rehabilitation, rather than a long-term stay. Use the tips in this chapter to make sure your parent is getting the most from their time in the nursing home. Listen carefully and ask plenty of questions during the assessment meetings. Talk with their therapists so you can help them with their therapy during your visits. Stay involved. Don't let the pain of seeing your parent disabled keep you away from them. Make it your job to see that your parent knows that they are in a nursing home for a purpose – to get better!

Chapter 8

Hospice, Death, and Funerals

Bring up the subject of a hospice and most people want to head in the other direction. It's kind of a taboo subject, one that conjures up images of dark smelly rooms filled with bone-thin, sick patients, waiting to die. But once you go through the hospice experience with a parent or relative, you may find it helps you overcome your fear of death and other fears you've been hiding from. You may find a hospice to be a beautiful, completely natural place. After all, we all die sometime. Why all the taboo about death? A hospice offers comfort and grace to the dying person. You'll usually find the doctors, nurses, social workers, ministers, and other people connected with a hospice are very open and direct when they speak with you. They don't beat around the bush like the doctors and technicians you've dealt with in the hospitals, nursing homes, and other places that cared for your parent.

I was at work when I received a disturbing call from my mom's doctor. Apparently her board and care owner had taken her to the doctor because she hadn't been drinking enough water and was dehydrated. The doctor called me to get permission to hydrate her. After a lot of beating around the bush, he finally told me that he wanted to inject a saline solution into her arm, not just give her a glass of water. But why call me at work about this? He kept saying something like "families have their own rules about this." I was astounded and perplexed! Did he expect me to just let Mom die from lack of water? It wasn't as if she was in the middle of the desert. Deep down within me (somewhere in deep-denial land), I had a suspicion that something else was going on – but I didn't know what. I asked the doctor if this was a one-time injection of water or if we'd have to bring Mom in on a weekly basis to put water into her veins. The doctor, probably now sensing that I was getting the drift of the conversation,

"Deep down within me (somewhere in deep-denial land), I had a suspicion that something else was going on – but I didn't know what."

assured me it was a one-time shot. Then the doctor closed the conversation by hinting that I should consider a hospice for my mom. That's when my denial met reality.

I was still in denial after the doctor mentioned the word "hospice" until it was brought up once again by the manager of the board and care facility where my mom was living. The director had seen many times the beginning signs of a person shutting down. She pointed out that Mom was eating and drinking less and less, and even clenching her teeth when efforts were made to spoon in more food or water. Ever the skeptic, I went there myself at dinner time and tried to coax Mom to eat more. My sister did too, and one night committed the *faux pas* of telling Mom that if she didn't eat more, she'd have to go back to the hospital. The next day Mom pulled me aside, and though she could barely talk without great effort, she made me promise I would never take her back to the hospital. When I looked into her eyes I knew what she was really saying. I couldn't exactly hear it, but I could sense it, even through my deep denial. I knew she had made her choice and I had been assigned to abide by it. That was the day I signed her up for a hospice.

What is a Hospice?

A hospice offers a way to die with dignity. It provides assistance to keep a dying person comfortable while letting the natural process of dying take place.

In a hospice, a person with a life-limiting illness is cared for in a comfortable surrounding, preferably a home. Medication is usually only dispensed for the patient's comfort. This can include medication for pain, nausea, vomiting, anxiety, depression, or any disorder causing the patient discomfort. Hospice workers are there for everything from backrubs and foot massages to morphine drips. There are even volunteers who come from the community to provide respite or companionship for hospice patients.

"Basically, a hospice is a place a person can die with dignity in a comfortable and loving environment, away from machines, lab technicians, hospital food, and harried nurses."

Most hospices have core services to help a dying patient. These are usually a registered nurse, social worker, chaplain, and a home health aide. Some hospices provide extra services such as homemakers and support groups to help the family. Hospice chaplains will perform memorial services if requested by the family. Basically, a hospice is a place a person can die with dignity in a comfortable and loving environment, away from machines, lab technicians, hospital food, and harried nurses.

While the emphasis is on comfort and not curing in a hospice, some people actually get better, and completely recover with all the attention they receive at a hospice. My aunt claims this happened to her.

Who Pays for Hospice Care?

In most cases it's paid for courtesy of Medicare for one 90-day period, followed by indefinite 60-day benefit periods. Your parent's HMO, Champus, or other private insurance plans may also pay. Hospices cannot decline service for lack of payment or source of insurance. There are non-profit and for-profit hospices. While both handle patients with and without insurance, the way they do so may differ. Some hospices are hybrids. They accept money from Medicare, private insurance, and community organizations.

Hospices Are Big Business

Call a few hospices to get an idea of their services and you'll probably be receiving calls back from a trained marketing staff that wants your business. You wouldn't think so, but hospices are a big-business industry. So there may be competition to provide hospice care for your parent. Competition can mean better service.

How Do You Find a Good Hospice?

A hospice recommendation usually comes from your parent's doctor, who determines when the time is right. He'll write an order for your parent to obtain hospice service. Hospice referrals are usually by word-of-mouth. You want to find a hospice with a good reputation, that's compassionate, free with the pain medication, and has other needed services to provide the family. If your doctor doesn't recommend a hospice, the care facility or the hospital caring for your parent may be able recommend one. Or perhaps a friend can recommend one.

This form included on the disk in the back of this book.

You'll want to shop around. Don't be sold on the very first one. If you're not emotionally ready to make a rational choice on the best hospice, don't be talked into enrolling your parent in a program just because you received a lot of calls from a nice salesman named Slick. To help you evaluate a hospice, please refer to the Hospice Checklist shown in Figure 8-1.

Once you have a few referrals, call them and talk with the nurse at the hospice referral desk to find out if the benefits they provide meet the needs of your parent and your family. Each hospice will have its own philosophy. Make sure their general philosophy agrees with yours.

Hospice Checklist

Does the hospice provide:

❑ Phone calls to the family?

❑ Mailings to the family on what to expect?

❑ Support groups?

❑ Retreats for the family?

❑ Activities for the family?

❑ Final arrangement support?

❑ Bereavement follow-up?

❑ A pastor or chaplain?

❑ Straight talk or summary from hospice nurse?

❑ Social Worker?

❑ Check-in assessment from a qualified nurse?

❑ Once-a-day nurse visits if needed?

❑ Every-other-day nurse visits if needed?

❑ Once-a-week nurse visits if needed?

❑ Home health aide on duty 24 hours a day if needed?

❑ Home health aide on duty 12 hours a day if needed?

❑ Do they provide any services at no charge?

❑ Do they accept Medicare?

❑ Do they accept Medicaid?

Figure 8-1 Hospice Checklist

Signing Up for a Hospice

Once you decide on a hospice, they'll usually send an admittance nurse over to evaluate you and your parent. They will perform a quick exam to check your parent's vital signs. If you're taking care of your parent, they'll ask you some general questions about your parent's health such as frequency of urination, color of urine, amount of food and water intake, etc. The admittance nurse, with a doctor's orders, then determines if it's appropriate to admit your parent to the hospice. Basically, she tries to determine if the shutdown phase of life has started. Also, she will determine if the family really wants to start hospice services, because it's ultimately up to the family, not the doctor, to begin this service.

If the admittance nurse determines that your parent can be admitted, she will have your parent or you (if you're the responsible party) sign the admittance papers. For me, this was when the real guilt began. Even though I was abiding by Mom's wishes when I admitted her into the hospice, I felt as though I was pulling a black hood over my head and becoming her executioner. I felt like I had signed her death warrant. I realized she would no longer be kept alive by any drugs, surgical procedures, or even simple injections of food or water. Admitting my parent to the hospice was saying it was OK for her to die. This is very difficult to do if you've been taking care of your parent from the start. There is always something inside you that just doesn't want to give up, something that's reaching for a miracle. Maybe the miracle is when you finally overcome your denial and abide by your parent's wishes instead of your own. Signing the physical form for admittance to a hospice is easy. Registering in your heart that you've signed it takes a while to accept. When you have to do it you might want to think carefully, as I did, if there's any alternative?

"I felt like I had signed her death warrant. I realized she would no longer be kept alive by any drugs, surgical procedures, or even simple injections of food or water."

Before your parent officially enters a hospice, or the final phase of life, you'll need to consult their life directives and death directives forms shown in Chapter 3. You'll also want to consider a Do Not Resuscitate Order (DNR) like the one shown in Figure 8-2. A DNR isn't required for the hospice. Many families have a hard time with this form. If your family is in this camp, I would recommend you speak to your hospice team about the form. It's also important you have your Power of Attorney for Health Care. Usually the hospice will want to keep copies of both these forms in their files.

This form included on the disk in the back of this book.

Meet the Hospice Nurse and Get the Straight Story

One of the goals of a hospice is to have a patient in hospice care before they're immediately dying. That way everyone knows each other and can work as a team. After you sign admittance papers for a hospice, you'll usually have a scheduled interview with your hospice nurse, who will go over the real reasons your parent is in the hospice. At this time you may learn everything involving your parent's health that their doctors wouldn't talk with you about. You'll get the low-down on why everyone in the hospital or nursing home made excuses when you asked them for specific answers about your parent's health.

The hospice nurse is used to death and dying. It's her specialty, and you'll usually find she's trained to help you handle it as well as possible. I felt the hospice nurse was like a guide, holding a light to show the way into a dark, scary cave we were entering. My sister and I had really never experienced death up close, but we were determined to stick with Mom to the end. The hospice nurse explained, in a matter-of-fact way, what everything would look and sound like as our mom's various organs began to shut down and death approached.

Use This Time to Plan for the Future

When your parent enters a hospice, you should start planning for the future. You probably don't want to think of that future, which is exactly why you should start planning for it now.

Do Not Resuscitate Order (DNR)

I _____ request limited emergency care as herein described.

I understand DNR means that if my heart stops beating or if I stop breathing, no medical procedure to restart breathing or heart functioning will be instituted.

I understand that this decision will not prevent me from obtaining other emergency medical care by pre-hospital emergency care personnel and/or medical care directed by a physician prior to my death.

I understand I may revoke this directive at any time either verbally or in writing.

I give permission for this information to be given to the pre-hospital emergency care personnel, doctors, nurses and other health personnel as necessary to implement this directive.

Being of sound mind, I voluntarily agree to this DNR order.

_____   _____
(Patient/Surrogate)   (Date)

_____
(Type or print patient's/surrogate full name)

_____   _____
(Signature of person who signed for declarant, if applicable)   (Date)

_____ _____
(Type or print full name)

ATTESTATION OF WITNESSES

The individual who has executed this order appears to be of sound mind, and under no duress, fraud or undue influence. Upon executing this order, the individual has (has not) received an identification bracelet.

_____

_____   _____
(Witness Signature)   (Date)

_____   _____
(Witness Signature)   (Date)

_____   _____
(Type or print witness's name)   (Type or print witness's name)

****

I affirm this directive is the expressed wish of the patient/surrogate, is medically appropriate, and a copy of this form is in the patient's permanent medical record.

In the event of cardiac or respiratory arrest, no chest compressions, assisted ventilations, intubation, defibrillation, or cardiotonic medications are to be initiated.

_____   _____
Physician's signature   Date

_____   _____
Address   Phone number

Figure 8-2 Sample Do Not Resuscitate Order (DNR)

Planning will keep your mind in active mode and take you away from dwelling on the inevitable. This is the time you need to start thinking of how you plan to carry out your parent's final directives. Do they want to be buried in the family burial plot located some distance away? Do they want to be cremated and their ashes spread in some exotic place, or carried into space? This is the time to start formulating a plan as to how you're going to do your best to carry out those wishes.

Consider who you would like to lead the memorial service and where you would like it held. If your parent was an active church member, you may want to have a service at their church. They were probably close to God there. If your parent wasn't active in a church you'll have to get creative. Your hunt for a memorial or funeral service venue should probably start with the number of people you expect to attend. If it will be over 30, you may want to consider a place other than a private residence. Usually there are people on staff at the hospice who can help you make these arrangements. Consult the Service Planning Checklist at the end of this chapter.

Changes That Appear as Death Approaches

The body has certain procedures it follows as it prepares for shutdown. While these symptoms don't happen all at once and don't happen to everyone, there is usually a pattern. Though everyone has their own personal method of dying, there are certain changes, both mental and physical, that take place. If you're observant you'll recognize them in your parent. And you'll have a start on preparing yourself for saying the final good-bye.

When someone dies from congestive heart failure, or a "natural death," the dying part is nothing like the blissful way Hollywood portrays death. Old people don't say their final, meaningful, words and then close their eyes and fall asleep. Dying from natural causes can be a long process, sometimes lasting months. There are obvious signs that tell you the end is approaching.

Physical Changes

You may notice a change in your parent's breathing pattern that initially looks pretty scary. They may breathe many shallow breaths and then not breathe for up to 30 seconds. You may even think they've passed away, but while you're running around trying to find a nurse, as I did, they'll start the short breaths again. This unusual type of breathing is called Cheyne-Stokes breathing. It's named after the person who first discovered it. Cheyne-Stokes breathing is caused by a decrease in circulation within the internal organs. Although it looks scary, it's very common. So common someone gave it his name.

"Though everyone has their own personal method of dying, there are certain changes, both mental and physical, that take place. If you're observant you'll notice them in your parent. And you'll have a start on preparing yourself for saying the final good-bye."

Older people tend to have poor circulation, so this symptom may actually go unnoticed. Their hands, arms, and feet will be cool to the touch and their skin color may actually change. Sometimes their fingernails will start to change color. This is a sign that blood circulation is decreasing, because the blood is going where it's most needed, to the vital organs. If this happens, keep your parent warm with an afghan or quilt.

Your parent may lose control of urine and/or bowel function as the muscles begin to relax. Although you can use adult diapers to control this, you should recognize it for what it is.

You parent may spend more time sleeping and be more difficult to wake up. This change is due to changes in the metabolism within the body. Sit with your parent patiently and hold their hand. Don't shout, crow like a rooster, or shake them to wake them up. Let them wake softly, as you would want to be wakened. Speak to them directly but softly, as you normally would. Be careful what you say when you think they're asleep. They may just be listening to you with their eyes closed.

Your parent may have almost no appetite and want less to drink. What is happening is that the body is conserving energy for more important tasks than processing food or drink. Usually, when a person no longer wants food or drink, it indicates they're getting ready for the final shutdown. They may even clench their teeth and refuse to take one more bite of food, as my mom did. If you try to fight this stage by threats or manipulation you usually end up regretting it. You can give them tiny bits of ice, a glycerin swab to cool their mouth, or a cool washcloth on the forehead. This is a good time to start saying your good-byes, and remind them how much they have meant to you, and how many good things you received from them in your life. Usually they'll know what's up, and be at peace with the decision. You may not be at peace with the decision, but you weren't in on the decision-making process.

"This is a good time to start saying your good-byes, and remind them how much they have meant to you, and how many good things you received from them in your life."

Psychological Changes

Your parent may pick or pull at invisible threads. These repetitive movements are a signal there's less oxygen going to their brain, causing metabolic changes. Don't try to correct these motions, just try and play some soothing music, or talk in a quiet or comforting tone.

Your parent may want to be alone more and have less to talk about. They may even withdraw completely and appear comatose. They may be confused about time, place, and people around them. Don't be alarmed. This is all part of the shutting down process. Speak clearly but softly, and don't be afraid to explain the reason for things, such as "James is here from Michigan to be with you," or "I'm going to put more medicine in your mouth to reduce the pain you're feeling." No matter how lost or out of it your parent may appear, be very careful what you say in their presence. Their hearing is normally the last thing to go. They may be listening to everything you say even when they appear not to be. Be positive in what you say and alert your family members to this fact. Don't ever discuss things you wouldn't want your parent to hear while in the room with them. Be kind and respectful at all times.

Your parent may speak, or claim to have spoken, to relatives or friends who have already died. Or they may see places you can't see. These visions will appear completely real to them. This experience is part of the transition they're making. Don't try to bring them back to your reality. Affirm their experience and give them your love.

Your parent may make an unusual request or say something that appears meaningless. But it may not be meaningless. This little statement or request may indicate he or she is ready to say good-bye but is testing you to see if you're ready to let go. Or they want to send you on a wild-goose chase for a good laugh. Although it may not make any sense to you at the time, accept any statement and grant any wish that you can without judgment or analysis. You'll have plenty of time for that later.

> "Your parent may make an unusual request or say something that appears meaningless. But it may not be meaningless."

Giving Permission to Go

If it hasn't happened by now, your parent may only want to be with one or two family members. Large groups may make them feel uncomfortable. This is usually a sign they're going inward and preparing to let go. If you're not part of this in crowd, it usually means you've fulfilled your job with your parent and it's time to say your good-byes. If you are part of the in-crowd, you'll need to give your parent affirmation, support, and permission to leave.

Your parent may have unresolved issues that make them linger, even while they're in pain. You can help them resolve these lingering or unresolved issues and let their spirit peacefully detach from their physical body. Your support and prayers can be what's needed to complete this unfinished business. Be there to offer support.

Don't make them feel they have to hang on because you still need them. Thank them over and over for their contribution to your life and give them permission to go. This may be hard but it's essential. You may want them to stay with you. Your mind convulses with all kinds of crazy reasons why you can't let them go. But it's real important now to give that permission. When a person is ready to die and you're able to be there for them, it's time to say good-bye out loud. Saying good-bye establishes closure and helps both of you make the final release possible. Tell them how much you'll miss them if necessary, but make closure. This is one of the greatest final offerings you can give your parent. You may want to take your parent's hand and recount childhood memories, forgive a long-held grudge, or whatever comes into your mind at their bedside. Most of all, be sure and thank them for all they've done for you. Now is the time to say it all. And crying is good too, even if you're a guy.

Signals That the End Is Very Near

Your parent may stare into space with a fixed gaze. If they haven't blinked in over five minutes, it's usually a sign they're drifting. Their consciousness may not be in their body but it's still be hovering in the room, so don't say anything you wouldn't want them to hear.

You may begin to hear gurgling noises coming from your parent's chest that sound like a coffee pot percolating. These sounds can become pretty loud during the last 24 hours of life. Hearing this, you'll understand where the term "death rattle" comes from. Even though this noise seems unusual, it's a normal transition due to the decrease in fluid intake and an inability to cough up mucus. After hearing this noise for a few hours, you may be tempted to ask the nurse to use as a medical suction device to clear the breathing. But suction won't really help. It will actually just create more mucus, which is what you don't want. Just use a tissue to wick away the fluid from the corner of your parent's mouth. Turn their head to help gravity drain the mucus. Be hygienic and use latex gloves when you touch saliva.

Generally, the rattle is a signal the end isn't far away, maybe even as close as 24 hours. At the first sign of the rattle, you'll want to make preparations to be at your parent's side when they pass away. You may want to get some sweatpants or comfortable clothes for sleeping, food and snacks, a cooler of cold drinks, and a sleeping bag. Staying until the end can be a once-in-a-lifetime experience. You may even find that your parent's death is one of the most beautiful and mystical experiences life offers you, almost as strange and mysterious as watching the birth of your own children.

> "You may want to get some sweatpants or comfortable clothes for sleeping, food and snacks, a cooler of cold drinks, and a sleeping bag. Staying until the end can be a once-in-a-lifetime experience."

Death is mysterious and picks its own timetable. Even though you're prepared to be there to the end and not let your parent die alone, you may head to the bathroom, only to find when you return that your parent chose that very moment to depart.

The Final Moment

When death finally comes, your parent's breathing will be slower and slower, until it finally stops. At this time you may catch a magical glimpse into what happens next. Close your eyes and let your imagination run free as you think of your parent and the journey their soul is taking. You may feel the presence of a long-lost friend or relative whose soul arrives to help them cross over. You may catch the feeling of God's love surrounding them. You may even get a glimpse of an angel in the room. Savor this personal, once-in-a-lifetime experience. Don't try to explain it to anyone – they'll probably never understand. But many people witness a remarkable event during a death of a loved one.

The moment of death of a parent is also an odd moment. You feel sad as you realize your parent has fulfilled their life on earth and will no longer be with you. At the same time you can't help but be awestruck by the whole death experience. Hopefully, by being there for your parent until the end, you'll feel no remorse or guilt. That doesn't mean you won't miss them. But you'll know you did your best for them and that's what they would have done for you. As you stand there alone in your feelings, with tears streaming down your face, you feel inside that your parent has gone to a better place where there is only love, and no pain.

You may also feel your own life has been changed by this event. Being present at the death of a parent has a strange way of putting your priorities in order. Your own mental outlook may be changed by witnessing your parent's death. Things that seemed important, such as job, career, and getting material things may no longer be as important as you once thought. Other responsibilities, such as being there for your family, may take on a higher priority.

> "You may also feel your own life has been changed by this event. Being present at the death of a parent has a strange way of putting your priorities in order. Your own mental outlook may be changed by witnessing your parent's death. Things that seemed important, such as job, career, and getting material things may no longer be as important as you once thought."

Getting Through the Details After the Final Moment

By this time someone in your family or a hospice worker has probably called the mortuary or cremation house that will take of your parent's body. If someone else is still there, you may want to leave before the undertakers arrive. I remember the appearance of the undertakers on my mom's fateful day. They seemed the strangest of the people that appeared that day. Wearing way too much aftershave, they worked unusually hard to be polite and kept nodding their heads like birds, while offering us their condolences.

The undertakers may not arrive in a black suits. They may not even drive a hearse. In our case, they arrived in an old beat-up van. But whatever they arrive in, their arrival tells you it's time to gather your clan and head over to the outdoors, coffee shop, or bar, depending on your preferences. You've been through an ordeal, and now you should be there for each other.

Post-Death Checklist

❑ Take all your parent's belongings from the building. This may include jewelry, false teeth, purse, clothes, etc. Nice things sometimes vanish fast.

❑ Call relatives and friends. Get help with this and divide the list among all of you. It's never pleasurable to deliver bad news. You can usually make everyone you contact feel better if you can tell them you were there when your parent died and that they went peacefully.

❑ Write an obituary for local newspapers. Go through your parent's scrapbook. Find out the important events in their life, and how they contributed to make life better for others. Pull together their Obituary Checklist from Chapter 3. Refine and enrich the obituary. This is a rewarding process, and you may learn things about your parent you never knew. Include the time and address of the service in the obituary so your parent's relatives and friends in the community can attend. Call the obituary editor at your local newspaper and find out what's required.

❑ While you have the old pictures out, collect a few you feel really capture your parent's essence and use them with your computer's word processor to write an invitation to the service. You can print these out and use them to invite family and friends of your parent to the service.

❑ Cancel services such as meals-on-wheels, home health agency aides, or volunteers. Tell them when the service will be, as they may have gotten to know your parent and want to attend.

❑ Check up on any animals. If your parent lived alone, you may have inherited a pet.

❑ Go to your parent's house and put timers on the lights and the TV. You don't want someone vandalizing or robbing their home before their affairs can be handled.

❑ Maintain their yard. You don't want it to show neglect and look as though someone isn't living there anymore.

❑ Collect the mail and file a change of address to your address. There may still be important mail arriving for the next three months.

❑ Stop any newspaper subscription unless you want to pick it up everyday. Nothing shouts that no one is home like unopened newspapers on the front lawn.

❑ Notify the Social Security Administration of the death at (800) 772-1213. Call any other pension or retirement services your parent may have been receiving benefits from. Most of them have a small death benefit.

❑ Call the cremation service or mortuary and order at least six death certificates. Certificates of death will be required for:

- credit card agencies
- Veteran's Administration
- pension

- life insurance
- banks
- others you haven't thought of

Figure 8-3 Post-Death Checklist

Once together, you can talk over good times, and start planning your parent's memorial or funeral service according to their wishes.

If you're going to have a funeral or burial service you'll want to start making the arrangements right away. If you'll be doing a cremation memorial, you can wait for a convenient time. Figure 8-3 shows a checklist of the things that need to be done after a death.

This form included on the disk in the back of this book.

Crematoriums offer the do-it-yourselfer control over the whole memorial process. You drive there, you pick up a kilo of ashes and you are left to your own devices to plan and conduct a service.

If your parent hasn't specified an exact mortuary or crematorium, use the checklist shown in Figure 8-4 to get some ideas on how to evaluate the costs and find one you're comfortable with.

This form included on the disk in the back of this book.

Planning a Funeral or Memorial Service

The difference between a funeral and a memorial depends on whether the deceased's remains are at the service or not. If your parent's remains will be at the service, it's normally referred to as a funeral. If you're having your parent's body cremated, you'll probably have a memorial service.

Mortuary Services

A mortuary can provide final arrangements for the body, including refrigeration, embalming or cremating. Some states require special permission from the family before allowing embalming, so refrigeration has gained favor in recent years. If for some reason the funeral is delayed, refrigeration may end up costing more than embalming. If the costs are comparable, embalming is the advised way to go since you have more options available if there is a delay in the memorial service. If you are planning a viewing of the body at the funeral, or shipping the body across state lines, embalming is almost always a necessity.

Caskets, burial vaults, and grave liners range in price from $500 to $7,000. Most take great pains to seal out the elements. The grave stone or grave site marker varies in cost depending on the size, material, and amount of detail carved into the stone. Prices usually start around $300 for a headstone. Then there is the plot of cemetery where the burial is to take place. Cemetery plots range in price like real estate plots. Normally you can figure on at least $1,000.

Cremation can be done at a mortuary or contracted out by the mortuary to a crematorium. There the body is placed in a cardboard box and burned at kiln temperatures. Cremated remains can be memorialized in many ways: ground burial, indoor or outdoor columbarium, or at private memorials. For cremation you can go through a mortuary, or for the cheapest route contact the crematorium directly. It's time to start considering options when your parent enters hospice.

Mortuary and Crematorium Costs

Mortuary Costs

Cost for refrigeration $_____   Cost for embalming $_____   Cost for rental of mortuary for service $_____

Cost for casket $_____   Cost for headstone $_____   Cost for mortuary cemetery $_____

Crematorium Costs

Cost for cremation $_____   Cost for urn $_____   Cost for rental of facility for service $_____

Figure 8-4 Mortuary and Crematorium Checklist

If desired, you can mix and match. Have an open casket for the public service and then have the body cremated and hold your own private service with the ashes. If there are other family members buried at a particular cemetery, you can include your parent's ashes next to their relatives' remains. It is sometimes nice to have a "resting place" where you can go to talk to your parent after their body has passed from this earth. For some people, a mortuary offers a favorable venue. Others may prefer to have ashes stored in an urn at home. It's all a matter of what your parent preferred, or if they left it to you, what you and your family are comfortable with.

Crematorium

These are typically small operations that pick up your parent's body at death and provide you with the ashes at a later date. Some have their own chapels that can be rented for a small fee. Typical cost for cremation ranges from $400 to $900.

If your parent was an active member of a church, you're in luck, as the church can be a great help in planning the service and offering the church as a place for the service. All that's required of you, aside from a donation, is writing the obituary mentioning the service and inviting family and friends to come. For the obituary draw your facts from the Personal Fact Sheet in Chapter 3. Contact your local paper's obituary editor and provide him with your facts and write up.

If your parent was a free spirit who didn't regularly attend church, or wasn't even baptized, you should think about having your own service. Try and keep the service in line with your parent's death directive as in Chapter 3. This should give you an outline, but you'll still need a venue. Remember, you don't need to have the service at a church for it to be official. Your parent's spirit is with God now. If they haven't left specific instructions on where they'd like their service to be, it's up to you. Get creative. Don't forget most states won't let you spread your parent's ashes around without a permit. You can usually get this permit at the crematorium. Also remember you don't always need to scatter ashes or bury a body at a memorial service. Here are a few examples to consider:

Service Planning Checklist

How many people would you expect to attend your parent's funeral?

( ) 1-10   ( ) 11- 20   ( ) 21-40   ( )41 - 60

What are a few places in your community that would seat that number of people comfortably?

_____   _____

_____   _____

Which of these facilities are available in the time you have available for the service?

_____   _____

_____   _____

Which minister, if any, will perform the service? _____

What will the basic outline of the service be?

1. Seating/Music – approximate time:_____ to _____ (am) (pm)

2. Hymn – name of hymn or song(s)_____ approximate time:_____

3. Introduction – approximate time:_____

4. Speech by minister – approximate time:_____

5. Speech by children – approximate time:_____

6. Open speech by participants – approximate time:_____

7. Closing speech – approximate time:_____

What visual aids will you present to remind participants of your parent?

1. Photos   _____ _____ _____ _____

2. Artwork   _____ _____ _____ _____

3. Favorite items_____ _____ _____ _____

Figure 8-5 Service Planning Checklist

• If your parent was an avid golfer, consider the golf course at his favorite hole. Imagine the minister arriving on a golf cart.

• If your parent was an avid fisherman, consider chartering a boat in their honor. You can scatter the ashes and head to their favorite fishing spot to fish in their honor.

• Most retirement homes have a small chapel they'll rent for a small amount (less than $50). If most of your parent's friends live in the same retirement home, it can become a convenient venue.

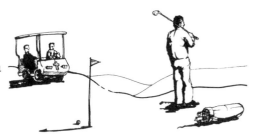

"If your parent was an avid golfer, consider the golf course at his favorite hole. Imagine the minister arriving on a golf cart."

This form included on the disk in the back of this book.

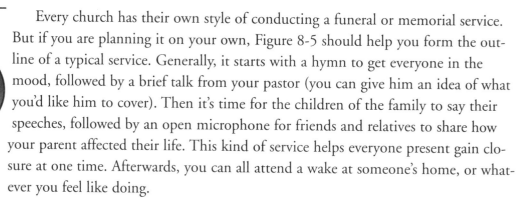

Every church has their own style of conducting a funeral or memorial service. But if you are planning it on your own, Figure 8-5 should help you form the outline of a typical service. Generally, it starts with a hymn to get everyone in the mood, followed by a brief talk from your pastor (you can give him an idea of what you'd like him to cover). Then it's time for the children of the family to say their speeches, followed by an open microphone for friends and relatives to share how your parent affected their life. This kind of service helps everyone present gain closure at one time. Afterwards, you can all attend a wake at someone's home, or whatever you feel like doing.

At this stage, you have completed caring for your parent. Now you have to deal with the trusts, distribution of the assets (if any), and keeping what's left of your family together in the period after your parent's passing. Do your best to stay in touch with everyone and hopefully the emotional closeness and the sharing of your intimacy will drive away the demons of depression. Hopefully, this experience will make your family circle tighter, and your life more enriched, ethical, and fullfilled, as in your heart, you know you did everything possible in helping your aging parent.

CHAPTER 9

Using the Disk in the Back of This Book

Inside the back cover of this book you'll find a compact disk with the sample forms shown in this book. These include checklists and other forms to help you with helping your aging parent. To use the forms you'll need either a Macintosh or IBM-style computer.

Accessing the Forms

Each form is available in two computer formats, Adobe Acrobat for opening with Adobe Acrobat Reader, and Rich Text for opening with a word processor.

Acrobat forms can be opened with Acrobat Reader. If you don't have Adobe Acrobat Reader installed on your computer, you can download a free version by turning your Web browser to www.adobe.com and following the instructions for downloading Adobe Acrobat Reader. Forms opened in Acrobat Reader cannot be edited. But if you don't have a word processor on your computer you can print out the forms and fill them in by hand.

Rich Text forms can be opened with a variety of word processing programs and can be customized for your use. When you're done, print out the form and use it as a checklist, or take it with you to the doctor's office, hospital, or when evaluating nursing homes. You can also save the form in a folder on the hard drive of your computer for future use.

Since each computer's font and margin settings may be slightly different, you should check your form for formatting before printing. You may have to make slight formatting changes to make the forms print neatly on the right number of pages, The Rich Text forms are set in Arial so they will appear correctly on as many computers as possible, but there may be variations of Arial type on different computers.

The forms will not auto-load onto your computer. We don't want to clutter your hard drive with forms you may not want. To load the forms you need from the CR-ROM, either open it as a document in your word processing program, or load it as an Adobe Acrobat file in Acrobat Reader and print it.

To use a form off the CD-ROM with Adobe Acrobat Reader

If you don't have a word processing program on your computer, you can print out and use the forms saved in Adobe Acrobat. They'll be formatted and ready to use. You won't be able to make changes to them, and you won't be able to save any changes. But you can print them out and fill them in by hand.

1. Place the CD-ROM from the back of this book in your CD-ROM drive and close the tray.

Scroll down the list of folders until you locate your CD-ROM drive. It will be the drive with the "Forms&Checklists" folder name in it..

2. With an IBM-type computer, click on Start, go to Programs, then Windows Explorer. Scroll down the list of folders until you locate your CD-ROM drive. It will be the drive with the "Forms&Checklists" folder name in it.

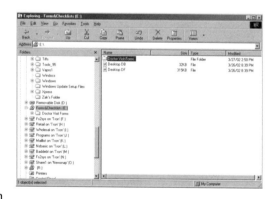

3. Double-click on the "Forms&Checklists" folder to open it.

4. Select the folder that has the subject of the forms you need by double-clicking on it.

Double-click on the "Forms&Checklists" folder to open it.

5. Select the form you need and open by double-clicking on it.

6. Select the format (in this case PDF) you need by double-clicking on it.

7. To view the form, double-click on it. This should automatically start Adobe Acrobat Reader and open the form. If it doesn't, you may need to load a free copy of Adobe Acrobat Reader to your computer from the Web site at www.adobe.com.

Click on Look In and scroll down until you find the CD-ROM with Forms&Checklists on it. Double-click on it.

Select the Rich Text (RTF) folder by double-clicking on it.

To use a form off the CD-ROM with your word processing program:

1. Put the CD-ROM from the back of this book in your CD-ROM drive and close the tray.

2. Start your word processing program, such as Microsoft Word

3. Click on File.

4. Click on Open.

5. Click on Look In and scroll down until you find the CD-ROM with Forms&Checklists on it. Double-click on it.

6. Select the folder that has the subject area you need by double-clicking on it.

7. Select the Rich Text (RTF) folder by double-clicking on it.

8. Select the form you need by double-clicking on it or clicking OPEN on your word processing software.

On a Macintosh

On a Macintosh-style computer, find the CD icon on your desktop. Double-click on the CD-ROM icon. Double-click on the Forms&Checklist folder. Double-click on the folder with the subject area you seek. Then double-click on either the Rich Text folder to start your word processor, or on the Adobe Acrobat folder to open the forms in Adobe Acrobat Reader.

Saving So You Can Find the Form for Next Time

Create a folder on the hard drive of your computer for saving these forms, as you won't be able to save changes onto the CD-ROM. You might want to call the folder something like "Mom's folder" or "Dad's folder." That way you'll have the forms in one spot when you need them in the future.

Notes

_____

_____

_____

_____

_____

_____

_____

_____

_____

_____

_____

_____

_____

_____

_____

_____

_____

_____

_____

_____

_____

_____

_____

_____

_____

_____

_____

Index

Other Practical References

Get A Life -
You Don't Need A Million To Retire Well

If you are spending all your time working to save money – neglecting family, friends and your own health, you may want to take a look at this book. You'll see how many options may be awaiting you in the area of life after work. See examples of what others have done with their lives in forming part-time businesses, volunteering, or just enjoying life in a different way than working every day. Includes chapters on what will you do when you retire, how to improve your health, how to get the most from your family relationships, the importance of friends, how to seek out others who have successfully retired, how to do your best to avoid nursing homes, how to estimate the money you'll need for retirement, figuring out where your money will come from after retirement, how to save enough, even if it appears impossible, and how to invest like a savvy retiree. **336 pages, 8 x 10, $24.95**

Beat the Nursing Home Trap

When taking care of your parent, there are many alternatives to expensive nursing homes – some you may have never heard of, or considered before. This consumer's guide to assisted living and long-term care facilities can show you little-known tricks and tips on getting the best care for the money you have to work with. It tells you how to seek help from others, how to assess your medical needs, laws regarding family leave, how to make a realistic family commitment, and how to find and evaluate a geriatric care manager. Also explains what you'll need as far as wills, living trusts, power of attorney and health care directives are concerned. Shows how to find different home care services, alternative methods of financing them, and supplemental care programs available. Covers independent and assisted living homes, nursing facilities, rules on asset protection and much more. If you are looking at alternatives to where your parent is currently living, you should have this book. **288 pages, 8 x 10, $21.95**

8 Ways to Avoid Probate

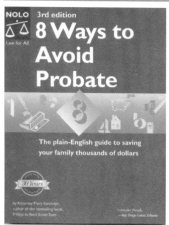

Probate can drag on for years, and the costs – including lawyer's fees, appraisal fees, court fees – can easily eat up thousands of dollars that would otherwise go to your family. With the help of this book you'll find 8 often-overlooked strategies for avoiding probate.

Includes how to set up a payable-upon-death account, how to name a beneficiary for a retirement account, naming a beneficiary for stocks and bonds, naming a beneficiary for vehicles, changing property to joint ownership, creating a living trust, taking advantage of special procedures for small estates, and making gifts as a way to avoid probate. Written in plain English by a lawyer who walks you through each step of the probate-avoidance process. **224 pages, 8 x 10, $19.95**

9 Ways to Avoid Estate Taxes

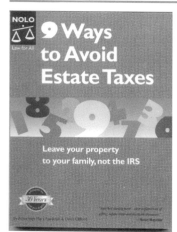

Estate taxes can be a rude awakening for even the most financially-savvy families. Estate taxes are currently charged on estates that exceed $675,000. With the price of real estate today, your parent's estate may be worth this, or more. And the taxes can be steep, with rates ranging from 37% to 55%.

This book explains how to shield as much of an estate as possible for family and other beneficiaries. Written by a lawyer, in plain English, it presents nine major methods that people can use to avoid or reduce federal estate taxes. These methods include: making gifts of under $10,000, making gifts for tuition or medical expenses, giving or leaving property to a spouse, creating a Bypass (AB) Trust, creating a QTIP or QDOT Trust, contributing to a charity, transferring life insurance policies, using disclaimers, and using special rules for small businesses. **240 pages, 8 x 10, $29.95**

Make Your Own Living Trust

By creating a living trust, a person can prevent lengthy and expensive probate hassles upon their death. A well-constructed and complete living trust is probably the best gift a person can leave behind for their family, as it helps the surviving family save time, money, and hassles.

With this easy-to-understand book you'll find how to create a probate-avoidance or tax-saving AB trust. You'll learn how to transfer all assets to a trust, including real estate, stocks, jewelry, art or a small business. You'll learn how to name beneficiaries. You'll get tips on how to find someone to manage trust property left over to children. You'll see how to provide for trust property management. You'll learn how to retain control over the trust property while you're still alive, and amend or change your trust at any time without having to pay a lawyer. Includes a FREE CD-ROM with the forms you need to help you or your parent set up a completely legal living trust. **345 pages, 8-1/2 x 11, $39.99**

Social Security, Medicare & Government Pensions

Everyone wants to get the most in retirement and pension income, as well as the best medical coverage. This book tells you how to apply for all the programs you're eligible for: retirement and disability programs, dependents and survivor benefits, supplemental security income, and veterans benefits. You'll see what you need to qualify, how to apply for Medicare and Medicaid, and how to combine Medicare with an HMO or managed health plan. Understand how to claim government pensions that you have earned.

With the help of this book you can plan your retirement ahead of time by making sure you have all your "ducks in a row" when it comes to your retirement benefits. Most people don't know which health insurance choice to make upon retiring. Here you'll find solid advice on whether you should choose a managed care plan, Medicare, a combination of both, or "medigap" coverage. This book can save you tons of money at a time when you'll need it most. **294 pages, 8-1/2 x 11, $29.99**

Order on a 10-Day Money Back Guarantee